10870431

Visions of the Afterlife

Visions of the Afterlife

COMPILED BY

CONSTANCE AND DANIEL POLLOCK

WORD PUBLISHING

NASHVILLE

A Thomas Nelson Company

WORD PUBLISHING

Copyright © 1999
by Constance Pollock and Daniel Pollock

No portion of this book may be reproduced, stored in a retrieval
system, or transmitted in any form or by any means—
electronic, mechanical, photocopy, recording, or any other—
except for brief quotations in printed reviews, without
the prior written permission of the publisher.

All scripture quotations are taken from
the King James Version of the Bible.

Library of Congress Cataloging-in-Publication Data
Visions of the afterlife / compiled by
Constance and Daniel Pollock.

p.   cm.

Includes bibliographical references and index.

ISBN 0-8499-1575-9

1. Future life—Quotations, maxims, etc.   2. Heaven—
Quotations, maxims, etc.   3. Hell—Quotations, maxims, etc.
I. Pollock, Constance, 1949–   II. Pollock, Daniel, 1944–   .

PN6084.F89V57   1999

808.8'03829123–DC21   99-18534
                                                       CIP

Printed in the United States of America
9 0 1 2 3 4 5 6 7 8 BVG 9 8 7 6 5 4 3 2

Acknowledgments

Grateful acknowledgment is made to the following publishers who have given permission to reprint copyrighted material:

Random House, Inc., for "Arrival" from *Shaker, Why Don't You Sing?* by Maya Angelou. Copyright © 1983 by Maya Angelou. And for "Hell" from *W. H. Auden: Collected Poems by W. H. Auden,* edited by Edward Mendelson. Copyright © 1940 and renewed 1968 by W. H. Auden.

Harold Matson Co., Inc., for "Miriam's Miracle" from *The Nightmare* by C. S. Forester. Copyright © 1954 by C. S. Forester.

Henry Holt and Company, Inc., for "Lost in Heaven" from *The Poetry of Robert Frost.* Copyright © 1969 by Henry Holt and Company, Inc., and © 1970 by Lesley Frost Ballantine.

Harcourt Brace & Company for "The Day with a White Mark" from *Poems* by C. S. Lewis, copyright © 1964 by the executors of the estate of C. S. Lewis and 1992 by C. S. Lewis Pte Ltd. and Walter Hooper. Reprinted by permission of Harcourt Brace & Company. And for "The World's Last Night" from *The World's Last Night and Other Essays,* copyright © 1958 by C. S. Lewis and renewed 1968 by Arthur Owen Barfield. And for "Joy: Heaven's Serious Business" and "The Flower to the Root" from *Letters to Malcolm: Chiefly on Prayer* by C. S. Lewis, copyright © 1983 by the executors of the estate of C. S. Lewis. And for "Murder in the Cathedral" from *Murder in the Cathedral* by T. S. Eliot, copyright © 1935 by Harcourt, Brace & World, Inc., and (c) 1963 by T. S. Eliot. And for the three words ("Hell is oneself") from *The Cocktail Party* by T. S. Eliot, copyright © 1949 by T. S. Eliot.

HarperCollins Ltd. for the excerpt from *The Screwtape Letters* by C. S. Lewis. Copyright © 1942 by C. S. Lewis.

Liveright Publishing Corporation for "if there are any heavens" copyright 1926, 1954, © 1991 by the Trustees for the E. E. Cummings Trust. Copyright © 1985 by George James Firmage, from *Complete Poems: 1904–1962* by E. E. Cummings.

Viking Penguin, a division of Penguin Books USA, Inc., and Laurence Pollinger Ltd., and the Estate of Frieda Lawrence

Ravagli for "Paradise Re-Entered," "Evil Is Homeless," "Tabernacle," and "The Hands of God" by D. H. Lawrence from *The Complete Poems of D. H. Lawrence* by D. H. Lawrence, edited by V. de Sola Pinto & F. W. Roberts. Copyright © 1964, 1971 by Angelo Ravagli and C. M. Weekley, executors of the Estate of Frieda Lasrence Ravagli. And for the excerpt from "The Second Coming" from *A Portrait of the Artist as a Young Man* by James Joyce. Copyright 1916 by B. W. Huebsch. Copyright 1944 by Nora Joyce. Copyright © 1964 by the Estate of James Joyce.

Simon & Schuster for the excerpt from "The Second Coming" from *The Poems of W. B. Yeats: A New Edition,* edited by Richard J. Finneran. Copyright © 1924 by Macmillan Publishing Company, renewed 1952 by Bertha Georgie Yeats.

Every effort has been made by the editors to contact the owners of the copyrighted material in this book. If we have inadvertently failed to acknowledge anyone, we shall be glad to hear from them so appropriate acknowledgments may be included in any future edition

For my mother, Arlene Barr Worwa.

——C. P.

And for our children, Jane and Edward.

——D. P.

Father of Heaven!
May we by the assistance of thy holy spirit so conduct
ourselves on earth as to secure an eternity of happiness
with each other in thy heavenly kingdom.

—JANE AUSTEN

CONTENTS

	Acknowledgments	V
	Introduction	I
1	*"A Heaven in a Wild Flower"*	13
2	*"God Grows Above"*	49
3	*"Joy Is the Serious Business of Heaven"*	67
4	*"Me Immortalized, and You"*	87
5	*"Appareled in Celestial Light"*	105
6	*"Abandon Hope, All Who Enter Here"*	125
7	*"Eye Hath Not Seen, nor Ear Heard"*	155
8	*"A New Heaven and a New Earth"*	175
	Biographical Notes	213

INTRODUCTION

I never saw a moor,
I never saw the sea;
Yet know I how the heather looks,
And what a wave must be

I never spoke with God,
Nor visited in heaven;
Yet certain am I of the spot
As if the chart were given.

In this poem, with simple and quiet surety, the Belle of Amherst, Massachusetts, Emily Dickinson, points us to Heaven.

Unseen, unheard, this Heaven is palpably real to Dickinson.

And so for centuries the idea of Heaven—and, inescapably, Hell—has intrigued the world's great writers, expressed in poetry, plays, songs, novels, sermons, and essays.

This volume gathers the visions of Heaven and Hell created by such literary masters as Shakespeare, John Donne, Emily Brontë, Charles Dickens, George Eliot, Henry Wadsworth Longfellow, Julia Ward Howe, Rudyard Kipling, C. S. Lewis, Harriet Beecher Stowe, James Joyce, Maya Angelou, T. S. Eliot, and more.

Is Heaven a place like Earth? Some, like *Christina Rossetti,* think so.

Paradise

Once in a dream I saw the flowers
   That bud and bloom in Paradise;
   More fair are they than waking eyes
Have seen in all this world of ours.
And faint the perfume-bearing rose,
   And faint the lily on its stem,
And faint the perfect violet,
    Compared with them.

Shall we be busy in Heaven? *Rudyard Kipling* has a colorful answer.

L' Envoi

When Earth's last picture is painted, and the tubes
   are twisted and dried,
When the oldest colors have faded, and the youngest
   critic has died,
We shall rest, and, faith, we shall need it—lie down
   for an eon or two,
Till the Master of All Good Workmen shall set us
   to work anew!

And those that were good shall be happy: they shall sit

in a golden chair;
They shall splash at a ten-league canvas with brushes
  of comets' hair;
They shall find real saints to draw from—Magdalene,
  Peter, and Paul;
They shall work for an age at a sitting and never be
  tired at all!

How do you get to Heaven? *John Keats* knows.

As from the Darkening Gloom

As from the darkening gloom a silver dove
Upsoars, and darts into the Eastern light,
On pinions that naught moves but pure delight,
So fled thy soul into the realms above,
Regions of peace and everlasting love;
Where happy spirits, crown'd with circlets bright
Of starry beam, and gloriously bedight,
Taste the high joy none but the blest can prove.

What will heaven sound like? *Maya Angelou* listens in
for us.

Arrival

Angels gather.
The rush of mad air

cyclones through.
Wing tips brush the
hair, a million
strands
stand; waving black anemones.
Hosannahs crush the
shell's ear tender, and
tremble
down clattering
to the floor.
Harps sound,
undulate their
sensuous meanings.

Will we find our loved ones in Heaven? *John Bunyan,* in his *The Pilgrim's Progress,* answers that.

> There, also, we shall meet thousands and thousands that have gone before us to that place; none of them hurtful, but loving holy, everyone walking in the sight of God, and standing in his presence with acceptance forever.

Would there be a Heaven without angels? *Dante Alighieri,* a visionary eyewitness, gives us a glimpse of angelic grandeur.

And at that center, with their wings expanded,
   More than a thousand jubilant Angels saw I,
   Each differing in effulgence and in kind.
I saw there at their sports and at their songs
   A beauty smiling, which the gladness was
   Within the eyes of all the other saints.

How shall we behave in Heaven? Tips from *Mark Twain*.

Etiquette for the Afterlife

- Upon arrival in heaven do not speak to St. Peter until spoken to. It is not your place to begin.

- Wait patiently in the queue till it comes your turn to apply for a ticket. Do not look bored, and don't scratch your shin with your other foot.

- When applying for a ticket, avoid trying to make conversation. St. Peter is hard-worked and has no time for conversation. If you *must* talk, let the weather alone. St. Peter cares not a damn for the weather. And don't ask him what time the 4:30 train goes; there aren't any trains in heaven, except the through-trains for the other place, and the less information you get about them, the better for you.

- Leave your dog outside. Heaven goes by favor. If it went by merit, you would stay out and the dog would go in.

- Keep off the grass.

These masters of language and imagination can fly us to Heaven, to see and experience the life beyond. And with equal ease, they can plunge us into the fiery, bitterly cold, interior deep known as Hell.

> Why this is hell
> Nor am I out of it;
> Thinkst thou that I who
> Saw the face of God
> And tasted the eternal
> Joys of Heaven,
> Am not tormented with
> Ten thousand hells
> In being deprived of
> Everlasting bliss!
>
> —CHRISTOPHER MARLOWE
> (from *Dr. Faustus*)

Last and crowning torture of all the tortures of that awful place is the eternity of hell. Eternity! O, dread and dire word. Eternity! What mind of man can understand it? And remember, it is an eternity of pain. Even though the pains of hell were not so terrible as they are, yet they would beome infinite, as they are destined to last for ever. But while they are everlasting they are at the same time, as you know, intolerably intense, unbearably extensive. To bear even the sting of an insect for all eternity would be a dreadful torment. What must it be, then, to bear the manifold tortures of hell for ever? For ever! For all eternity! Not for a year or for an age but for ever.

—JAMES JOYCE
(from *A Portrait of the Artist as a Young Man*)

The Bible has been the wellspring of inspiration for many great writers. References to Heaven and Hell, scattered throughout the Scriptures, are collected here for a unique look at the life of the world to come. A few examples (from the King James Version, itself a masterpiece of literature):

They shall be abundantly satisfied with the fatness of thy house; and thou shalt make them drink of the river of thy pleasures. For with thee is the fountain of life: in thy light shall we see light.

—PSALM 36:8–9

For we know that if our earthly house of this tabernacle were dissolved, we have a building of God, an house not made with hands, eternal in the heavens. For in this we groan, earnestly desiring to be clothed upon with our house which is from heaven: If so be that being clothed we shall not be found naked. For we that are in this tabernacle do groan, being burdened: not for that we would be unclothed, but clothed upon, that mortality might be swallowed up of life. Now he that hath wrought

us for the selfsame thing is God, who also hath
given unto us the earnest of the Spirit.

—2 CORINTHIANS 5:1–5

Dead things are formed from under the waters,
and the inhabitants thereof. Hell is naked before
him, and destruction hath no covering.

—JOB 26:5–6

The Son of man shall send forth his angels, and
they shall gather out of his kingdom all things that
offend, and them which do iniquity; and shall cast
them into a furnace of fire: there shall be wailing
and gnashing of teeth.

—MATTHEW 13:41–42

Finally, with the ticking to the Millennium growing ever louder, who can ignore thoughts of the
afterlife? According to a *U.S. News & World Report* poll,
66 percent of Americans say they believe that Jesus
Christ will return to Earth, an increase from 61 percent three years ago. Jesus Himself promised it, and
the book of Revelation—with its glorious and awe-
some poetic vision—portends the destruction of the
world, to clear the way for "a new heaven and a new
earth" (21:1–14).

The powerful imagery, themes, and motifs of the
book of Revelation have long enthralled our greatest
writers. *Visions of the Afterlife* concludes by pairing literary and scriptural citations of the Apocalypse:

And one of the elders answered, saying unto me,
What are these which are arrayed in white robes?
and whence came they? And I said unto him, Sir,
thou knowest. And he said to me, These are they
which came out of great tribulation, and have
washed their robes, and made them white in the
blood of the Lamb. Therefore are they before the
throne of God, and serve him day and night in his
temple: and he that sitteth on the throne shall
dwell among them. They shall hunger no more,
neither thirst any more; neither shall the sun light
on them, nor any heat. For the Lamb which is in
the midst of the throne shall feed them, and shall
lead them unto living fountains of waters: and God
shall wipe away all tears from their eyes.

—REVELATION 7:13–17

General William Booth Enters Heaven
(Booth was the founder of the Salvation Army.)

(Bass drums beaten loudly.)
   Booth led boldly with his big bass drum—
   (Are you washed in the blood of the Lamb?)
   The Saints smiled gravely, and they said: "He's come."
   (Are you washed in the blood of the Lamb?)
   Walking lepers followed, rank on rank,
   Lurching bravos from the ditches dank,
   Drabs from the alleyways and drug fiends pale—
   Minds still passion-ridden, soul-powers frail:—

Vermin-eaten saints with moldy breath
Unwashed legions with the ways of Death—
(Are you washed in the blood of the Lamb?)

(Banjos.)

Every slum had sent its half-a-score
The round world over. (Booth had groaned for more.)
Every banner that the wide world flies
Bloomed with glory and transcendent dyes.
Big-voiced lassies made their banjos bang,
Tranced, fanatical, they shrieked and sang:—
("Are you washed in the blood of the Lamb?")

Hallelujah! It was queer to see
Bull-necked convicts with that land make free!
Loons with trumpets blowed a blare, blare, blare—
On, on, upward through the golden air!
(Are you washed in the blood of the Lamb?)

—VACHEL LINDSAY

For I testify unto every man that heareth the words of the prophecy of this book, If any man shall add unto these things, God shall add unto him the plagues that are written in this book: And if any man shall take away from the words of the book of this prophecy, God shall take away his part out of the book of life, and out of the holy city, and from the things which are written in this book. He which testifieth these things saith, Surely I come quickly. Amen. Even so, come, Lord Jesus.

—REVELATION 22:18–20

The Second Coming

Surely some revelation is at hand;
Surely the Second Coming is at hand.
The Second Coming! Hardly are those words out
When a vast image of *Spiritus Mundi*
Troubles my sight: somewhere in the sand of the desert
A shape with lion body and head of a man,
A gaze blank and pitiless as the sun,
Is moving its slow thighs, while all about it
Reel shadows of the indignant desert birds.
The darkness drops again; but now I know
That twenty centuries of stony sleep
Were vexed to nightmare by a rocking cradle,
And what rough beast, its hour come round at last,
Slouches toward Bethlehem to be born?

—WILLIAM BUTLER YEATS

Following the chapter on Revelation are capsule biographies of these writers who so eloquently imparted their visions of glorious Heaven and gory Hell.

In the end, we want to answer in the affirmative to Emily Dickinson, who pointedly asks: *"Going to Heaven! I don't know when . . . Perhaps you're going too!"*

—CONSTANCE AND DANIEL POLLOCK

CHAPTER 1
"A HEAVEN IN A WILD FLOWER"

William Blake could see "Heaven in a wild flower." And so it has been for many visionary writers—Heaven is viewed as an uncorrupted Earth, and nature, in all its beauties, as a looking glass into eternity. Other writers describe our future lives as an idealization of our terrestrial experience. Happiness? Certainly. Work? Completely fulfilling. Harps and halos? Let Mark Twain and C. S. Lewis enlighten you on these particulars.

CONCORD, Thursday—I had an early run in the woods before the dew was off the grass. The moss was like velvet, and as I ran under the arches of yellow and red leaves I sang for joy, my heart was so bright and the world so beautiful. I stopped at the end of the walk and saw the sunshine out over the wide "Virginia meadows."

It seemed like going through a dark life or grave into heaven beyond. A very strange and solemn feeling came over me as I stood there, with no sound but the rustle of the pines, no one near me, and the sun so glorious, as for me alone. It seemed as if I felt God as I never did before, and I prayed in my heart that I might keep that happy sense of nearness in my life.

—LOUISA MAY ALCOTT
(from the journals of Louisa May Alcott)

L' Envoi

When Earth's last picture is painted, and the tubes
    are twisted and dried,
When the oldest colors have faded, and the youngest
    critic has died,
We shall rest, and, faith, we shall need it—lie down
    for an eon or two,
Till the Master of All Good Workmen shall set us
    to work anew!

And those that were good shall be happy: they shall sit
    in a golden chair;
They shall splash at a ten-league canvas with brushes
    of comets' hair;
They shall find real saints to draw from—Magdalene,
    Peter, and Paul;
They shall work for an age at a sitting and never be
    tired at all!

And only the Master shall praise us, and only the Master
    shall blame;
And no one shall work for money, and no one shall work
    for fame;
But each for the joy of the working, and each, in his
    separate star
Shall draw the Thing as he sees It for the God of Things
    as They Are!

—RUDYARD KIPLING

The World

I saw Eternity the other night,
Like a great ring of pure and endless light,
   All calm as it was bright;
And round beneath it, Time, in hours, days, years,
   Driven by the spheres,
Like a vast shadow moved, in which the world
   And all her train were hurled.
The doting lover, in his quaintest strain,
   Did there complain;
Near him his lute, his fancy, and his flights,
   Wit's sour delights;
With gloves, and knots, the silly snares of pleasure,
   Yet his dear treasure,
All scattered lay, while he his eyes did pour
   Upon a flower.

The darksome statesman, hung with weights and woe,
Like a thick midnight fog, moved there so slow,
   He did not stay nor go;
Condemning thoughts (like sad eclipses) scowl
   Upon his soul,
And clouds of crying witnesses without
   Pursued him with one shout.
Yet digged the mole, and, lest his ways be found,
   Workt under ground,
Where he did clutch his prey; but one did see
   That policy;
Churches and altars fed him; perjuries
   Were gnats and flies;
It rained about him blood and tears; but he
   Drank them as free.

The fearful miser, on a heap of rust
Sat pining all his life there, did scarce trust
   His own hands with the dust;
Yet would not place one piece above, but lives
   In fear of thieves.
Thousands there were, as frantic as himself,
   And hugged each one his pelf;
The downright epicure placed heaven in sense,
   And scorned pretense;
While others, slipt into a wide excess,
   Said little less;
The weaker sort, slight, trivial wares enslave,
   Who think them brave;
And poor despised Truth sat counting by
   Their victory.

Yet some, who all this while did weep and sing,
And sing and weep, soared up into the ring;
   But most would use no wing.
"O fools," said I, "thus to prefer dark night
   Before true light!
To live in grots and caves, and hate the day
   Because it shows the way,—
The way which, from this dead and dark abode,
   Leads up to God;
A way where you might tread the sun and be
   More bright than he!"
But, as I did their madness so discuss,
   One whispered thus,
"This ring the Bridegroom did for none provide,
   But for his Bride."

—HENRY VAUGHAN

Auguries of Innocence

To see a World in a grain of sand,
And a Heaven in a wild flower,
Hold Infinity in the palm of your hand,
And Eternity in an hour.
A robin redbreast in a cage
Puts all Heaven in a rage.
A dove-house fill'd with doves and pigeons
Shudders Hell thro' all its regions
A dog starv'd at his master's gate
Predicts the ruin of the State.
A horse misus'd upon the road
Calls to Heaven for human blood.
Each outcry of the hunted hare
A fibre from the brain does tear,
A skylark wounded in the wing,
A cherubim does cease to sing.
The game-cock clipt and arm'd for flight
Does the rising sun affright.
Every wolf's and lion's howl
Raises from Hell a Human soul.
The wild deer, wandering here and there,
Keeps the Human soul from care.
The Lamb misus'd breeds public strife,
And yet forgives the butcher's knife.
The bat that flits at close of eve
Has left the brain that won't believe.
The owl that calls upon the night
Speaks the unbeliever's fright.
He who shall hurt the little wren

Shall never be belov'd by men.
He who the ox to wrath has mov'd
Shall never be by woman lov'd.
The wanton boy that kills the fly
Shall feel the spider's enmity.
He who torments the chafer's sprite
Weaves a bower in endless night.
The caterpillar on the leaf
Repeats to thee thy mother's grief.
Kill not the moth nor butterfly,
For the Last Judgement draweth nigh.
He who shall train the horse to war
Shall never pass the polar bar.

—WILLIAM BLAKE

On a Drop of Dew

See how the Orient dew,
    Shed from the bosom of the morn
    Into the blowing roses,
Yet careless of its mansion new;
For the clear region where 'twas born
    Round in its self incloses:
    And in its little globe's extent,
Frames as it can its native element.
    How it the purple flow's does slight,
        Scarce touching where it lies,
    But gazing back upon the skies,
        Shines with a mournful light;
            Like its own tear,
Because so long divided from the sphere.
    Restless it rolls and unsecure,

Trembling lest it grow impure:
    Till the warm sun pity its pain,
And to the skies exhale it back again.
        So the soul, that drop, that ray
Of the clear fountain of eternal day,
Could it within the human flow'r be seen,
            Rememb'ring still its former height,
            Shuns the sweet leaves and blossoms green;
            And, recollecting its own light,
Does, in its pure and circling thoughts, express
The greater heaven in an heaven less.
            In how coy a figure wound,
            Every way it turns away:
            So the world excluding round,
            Yet receiving in the day.
            Dark beneath, but bright above:
            Here disdaining, there in love,
            How loose and easy hence to go:
            How girt and ready to ascend.
            Moving but on a point below,
            It all about does upwards bend.
Such did the manna's sacred dew distil;
White, and entire, though congeal'd and chill.
Congeal'd on earth: but does, dissolving, run
Into the glories of th' almighty sun.

—ANDREW MARVELL

❧

Midnight

When to my eyes
(Whilst deep sleep others catches,)

Thine host of spies
The stars shine in their watches,
    I do survey
    Each busy ray,
And how they work, and wind,
    And wish each beam
    My soul doth stream,
With the like ardor shined;
    What emanations,
    Quick vibrations
And bright stars are there?
    What thin ejections,
    Cold affections,
And slow motions here?

Thy heavens (some say,)
Are a fiery-liquid light,
    Which mingling aye
Streams, and flames thus to the sight.
    Come then, my God!
    Shine on this blood,
And water in one beam,
    And thou shalt see
    Kindled by thee
Both liquors burn, and stream.
    O what bright quickness,
    Active brightness,
And celestial flows
    Will follow after
    On that water,
Which thy spirit blows!

—HENRY VAUGHAN

Hosanna

The Deity, the Deity to me
Doth all things give, and make me clearly see
    The moon and stars, the air and sun
      Into my chamber come;
    The seas and rivers hither flow,
    Yea, here the trees of Eden grow,
      The fowls and fishes stand,
        Kings and their thrones,
      As 'twere, at my command;
      God's wealth, his holy ones,
The ages too, and angels all conspire:
While I, that I the center am, admire.

No more, no more shall clouds eclipse my treasures,
Nor viler shades obscure my highest pleasures;
    No more shall earthen husks confine
      My blessings which do shine
    Within the skies, or else above:
    Both worlds one Heaven made by love,
      In common happy I
        With angels walk
      And there my joys espy;
      With God himself I talk;
Wondering with ravishment all things to see
Such real joys, so truly mine, to be.

No more shall trunks and dishes be my store,
Nor ropes of pearl, nor chains of golden ore;
    As if such beings yet were not,

They all shall be forgot.
No such in Eden did appear,
No such in Heaven: Heaven here
  Would be, were those removed;
    The sons of men
  Live in Jerusalem,
  Had they not baubles loved.
These clouds dispersed, the heavens clear I see.
Wealth new-invented, mine shall never be.

Transcendent objects doth my God provide,
In such convenient order all contrived,
  That all things in their proper place
    My soul doth best embrace,
  Extends its arms beyond the seas,
  Above the heavens its self can please,
    With God enthroned may reign;
    Like sprightly streams
  My thoughts on things remain,
  Even as some vital beams
They reach to, shine on, quicken things, and make
Them truly useful; while I All partake.

—THOMAS TRAHERNE

The Day with a White Mark

All day I have been tossed and whirled in a preposterous
  happiness:
Was it an elf in the blood! or a bird in the brain! or even
  part
Of the cloudily crested, fifty-league-long, loud uplifted
  wave

Of a journeying angel's transit roaring over and through
   my heart?

My garden's spoiled, my holidays are canceled, the
   omens harden;
The plann'd and unplann'd miseries deepen; the knots
   draw tight.
Reason kept telling me all day my mood was out of season.
It was, too. In the dark ahead the breakers only are white.

Yet I—I could have kissed the very scullery taps. The
   color of
My day was like a peacock's chest. In at each sense there
   stole
Ripplings and dewy sprinkles of delight that with them
   drew
Fine threads of memory through the vibrant thickness of
   the soul.

As though there were transparent earths and luminous
   trees should grow there,
And shining roots worked visibly far down below one's
   feet,
So everything, the tick of the clock, the cock crowing in
   the yard
Probing my soil, woke diverse buried hearts of mine to
   beat,

Recalling either adolescent heights and the inaccessible
Longings and ice-sharp joys that shook my body and
   turned me pale,
Or humbler pleasures, chuckling as it were in the ear,
   mumbling
Of glee, as kindly animals talk in a children's tale.

Who knows if ever it will come again, now the day closes?
No one can give me, or take away, that key. All depends
On the elf, the bird, or the angel. I doubt if the angel
　himself
Is free to choose when sudden heaven in man begins or
　ends.

—C. S. LEWIS

Heaven Is What I Cannot Reach!

Heaven is what I cannot reach!
　The apple on the tree,
Provided it do hopeless hang,
　That "heaven" is, to me.

The color on the cruising cloud,
　The interdicted ground
Behind the hill, the house behind,—
　There Paradise is found!

—EMILY ÐICKINSON

A Halo and a Harp

People take the figurative language of the Bible and
the allegories for literal, and the first thing they ask
for when they get here is a halo and a harp, and so
on. Nothing that's harmless and reasonable is
refused to a body here, if he asks it in the right spirit. So they are outfitted with these things without a
word. They go and sing and play just about one day,
and that's the last you'll ever see of them in the

choir. They don't need anybody to tell them that that sort of thing wouldn't make a heaven—at least not a heaven that a sane man could stand a week and remain sane. That cloud-bank is placed where the noise can't disturb the old inhabitants, and so there ain't any harm in letting everybody get up there and cure himself as soon as he comes.

Now you just remember this—heaven is as blissful and lovely as it can be; but it's just the busiest place you ever heard of. There ain't any idle people here after the first day. Singing hymns and waving palm branches through all eternity is pretty when you hear about it in the pulpit, but it's as poor a way to put in valuable time as a body could contrive. It would just make a heaven of warbling ignoramuses, don't you see? Eternal Rest sounds comforting in the pulpit, too. Well, you try it once, and see how heavy time will hang on your hands. Why, Stormfield, a man like you, that had been active and stirring all his life, would go mad in six months in a heaven where he hadn't anything to do. Heaven is the very last place to come to rest in,—and don't you be afraid to bet on that!

—MARK TWAIN

(Sam's advice to Captain Stormfield, a newcomer to heaven, from *Captain Stormfield's Visit to Heaven*)

Paradise

Once in a dream I saw the flowers
    That bud and bloom in Paradise;

More fair they are than waking eyes
Have seen in all this world of ours.
And faint the perfume-bearing rose,
    And faint the lily on its stem,
And faint the perfect violet,
    Compared with them.

I heard the songs of Paradise;
    Each bird satisfactory singing in its place;
    A tender song so full of grace
It soared like incense to the skies;
Each bird satisfactory singing to its mate
    Soft cooing notes among the trees;
        To such as these.

I saw the fourfold River flow,
And deep it was, with golden sand;
    It flowed between a mossy land
With murmured music grave and low.
It hath refreshment for all thirst,
    For fainting spirit strength and rest;
Earth holds not such a draught as this
    From east to west.

The Tree of Life stood budding there,
    Abundant with its twelvefold fruits;
    Eternal sap sustains its roots,
Its shadowing branches fill the air.
Its leaves are healing for the world,
    Its fruit the hungry world can feed,
Sweeter than honey to the taste
    And balm indeed.

I saw the Gate called Beautiful;

And looked, but scarce could look, within;
I saw the golden streets begin,
And outskirts of the glassy pool.
O harps, oh, crowns of plenteous stars,
O green palm branches, many-leaved—
Eye hath not seen nor ear hath heard,
Nor heart conceived.

I hope to see these things again,
But not as once in dreams by night;
To see them with my very sight,
And touch and handle and attain:
To have all heaven beneath my feet
For narrow way that once they trod;
To have my part with all the saints,
And with my God.

—CHRISTINA GEORGINA ROSSETTI

The Coming of Light

Birds, many-voiced, far through the forest sing;
Along the vale the mist winds like a stream,
But heaven's clearness broadens and strikes deep
Till bough and branchlet, new-bathed, upward spring
From gulfs of fragrance where all night they sleep.
All things take colour now before my eyes
And pearl-drops tremble on each leaf and flower.
The earth around me has grown Paradise.

Look up, look up! Far off the giant mountains
Foretell the coming of the sacred hour.
They take their joy in those eternal fountains

Ere yet the flood-light fall on us below.
In the high pastures all the dimpled hollows
Moment by moment bright and brighter grow,
And downward still the jewelled splendour follows.
The sun is here!—Alas, my eyes are blinded!
I turn away—I cannot bear his radiance.

Even so it is when all the self is minded
To force the goal by our own confidence,
And wide are flung the gates of all fulfilment;
Sudden there bursts from that eternal portal
A sea of flame—past mercy—past concealment.
We thought to light a candle—fire immortal
Wraps us, engulfed in unknown glowing seas.

—JOHANN WOLFGANG VON GOETHE
(from *Faust,* trans. by F. Melian Stawell)

The Spectacle

Scan with calm bloodshot eyes the world around us,
Its broken stones, its sorrows! No voice could tell
The toll of the innocent crucified, weeping and wailing,
In this region of torment ineffable, flame and derision—
  What wonder if we believe no longer in Hell?

  And Heaven! That daybreak vision?
In the peace of our hearts we learn beyond shadow of
  doubting,
That our dream of this vanished kingdom lies sleeping
  within us;
Its gates are the light we have seen in the hush of the
  morning,

When the shafts of the sunrise break in a myriad
    splendours;
Its shouts of joy are those of all earthly creatures,
Their primal and innocent language—the song of the
    birds: Thrush in its rapture, ecstatic wren, and wood-
    dove tender,
Calling on us poor mortals to put our praise into words.

Passionate, sorrowful hearts, too—the wise, the true and
    the gentle;
Minds that outface all fear, defy despair, remain faithful,
Endure in silence, hope on, assured in their selfless
    courage,
Natural and sweet in a love no affliction or doubt could
    dispel.

If, as a glass reflecting its range, we have these for our
    guidance,
If, as our love creates beauty, we exult in that transient
    radiance,
This is the garden of paradise which in our folly
        We abandoned long ages gone.

Though, then, the wondrous divine were ev'n nebulae-
    distant,
The little we make of our all is our earthly heaven.
        Else we are called in a darkness,
Windowless, doorless, alone.

—WALTER DE LA MARE

Going to Heaven!

Going to Heaven!
I don't know when—
Pray do not ask me how!
Indeed I'm too astonished
To think of answering you!
Going to Heaven!
How dim it sounds!
And yet it will be done
As sure as flocks go home at night
Unto the Shepherd's arm!

Perhaps you're going too!
Who knows?
If you should get there first
Save just a little space for me
Close to the two I lost—
The smallest "Robe" will fit me
And just a bit of "Crown"—
For you know we do not mind our dress
When we are going home—

I'm glad I don't believe it
For it would stop my breath—
And I'd like to look a little more
At such a curious Earth!
I'm glad they did believe it
Whom I have never found
Since the mighty Autumn afternoon
I left them in the ground.

—EMILY DICKINSON

The Flower

How fresh, O Lord, how sweet and clean
Are Thy returns! ev'n as the flowers in Spring,
To which, besides their own demesne,
The late-past frosts tributes of pleasure bring;
    Grief melts away
    Like snow in May
As if there were no such cold thing.

Who would have thought my shrivell'd heart
Could have recover'd greenness? It was gone
Quite under ground; as flowers depart
To see their mother-root, when they have blown;
    Where they together
    All the hard weather,
Dead to the world, keep house unknown.

These are Thy wonders, Lord of power,
Killing and quick'ning, bringing down to Hell
    And up to Heaven in an hour;
Making a chiming of a passing-bell
    We say amiss
    This or that is;
Thy word is all, if we could spell.

O that I once past changing were,
Fast in Thy Paradise, where no flower can wither;
    Many a spring I shoot up fair,
Off'ring at Heav'n, growing and groaning thither;
    Nor doth my flower
    Want a spring-shower,
My sins and I joining together.

    But while I grow in a straight line,

Still upwards bent, as if Heav'n were mine own,
  Thy anger comes, and I decline:
What frost to that? what pole is not the zone
    Where all things burn,
    When Thou dost turn,
And the least frown of Thine is shown?

And now in age I bud again,
After so many deaths I live and write;
I once more smell the dew and rain,
And relish versing: O, my only Light,
    It cannot be
    That I am he
On whom Thy tempests fell all night.

These are Thy wonders, Lord of love,
To make us see we are but flow'rs that glide;
    Which when we once can find and prove,
Thou hast a garden for us where to bide;
    Who would be more,
    Swelling through store,
Forfeit their Paradise by their pride.

—GEORGE HERBERT

To the Gate

And thus it was: I writing of the way
And race of saints in this our gospel-day,
Fell suddenly into an allegory
About the journey, and the way to Glory.

Come hither,
And lay my book, thy head and heart together

Now I saw in my dream that by this time the pilgrims were got over the Enchanted Ground, and entering into the country of Beulah, whose air was very sweet and pleasant, the way lying directly through it, they solaced themselves there for a season. Yea, here they heard continually the singing of birds, and saw every day the flowers appear in the earth. In this country the sun shineth night and day; wherefore this was beyond the Valley of the Shadow of Death, and also out of the reach of Giant Despair; neither could they from this place so much as see Doubting-Castle. Here they were within sight of the city they were going to: also here met them some of the inhabitants thereof. For in this land the Shining Ones commonly walked, because it was upon the borders of Heaven. In this land also the contract between the bride and the Bridegroom was renewed: Yea here, as the Bridegroom rejoiceth over the bride, so did their God rejoice over them. Here they had no want of corn and wine; for in this place they met with abundance of what they had sought for in all their pilgrimage. Here they heard voices from out of the City, loud voices, saying, Say ye to the daughter of Zion, Behold thy salvation cometh, behold his reward is with him. Here all the inhabitants of the country called them, The holy People, the redeemed of the Lord.

Now as they walked in this land they had more rejoicing than in parts more remote from the kingdom to which they were bound; and drawing near to the City, they had yet a more perfect view thereof. It was builded of pearls and precious stones, also the street thereof was paved with gold, so that by reason of the natural glory of the City, and the reflection of the sunbeams upon it, with desire fell sick, Hopeful also had a fit or two of the same disease: wherefore here they lay by it a whole, crying out because of their pangs, If you see my Beloved, tell him that I am sick of love.

—JOHN BUNYAN
(from *The Pilgrim's Progress*)

I Went to Heaven

I went to heaven,—
'T was a small town,
Lit with a ruby,
Lathed with down.
Stiller than the fields
At the full dew,
Beautiful as pictures
No man drew.
People like the moth,
Of mechlin, frames,
Duties of gossamer,
And elder names.
Almost contented
I could be
'Mong such unique
Society.

— EMILY ÐICKINSON

Hymn to God, My God, in My Sickness

Since I am coming to that holy room,
Where, with thy choir of saints for evermore,
I shall be made thy music; as I come
I tune the instrument here at the door,
And what I must do then, think here before.

Whilst my physicians by their love are grown
Cosmographers, and I their map, who lie
Flat on this bed, that by them may be shown
That this is my south-west discovery
Per fretum febris, by these straits to die,

I joy, that in these straits, I see my west;
For, though their currents yield return to none,
What shall my west hurt me? As west and east
In all flat maps (and I am one) are one,
So death doth touch the resurrection.

Is the pacific sea my home? Or are
The eastern riches? Is Jerusalem?
Anyan, and Magellan, and Gibraltar,
All straits, and none but straits, are ways to them,
Whether where Japhet dwelt, or Cham, or Sem.

We think that Paradise and Calvary,
Christ's Cross, and Adam's tree, stood in one place;
Look, Lord, and find both Adams met in me;
As the first Adam's sweat surrounds my face,
May the last Adam's blood my soul embrace.

So, in his purple wrapp'd receive me, Lord,
By these his thorns give me his other crown;
And as to others' souls I preach'd thy word,

Be this my text, my sermon to mine own,
Therefore that he may raise the Lord throws down.

—JOHN ĐONNE

Never a Tremor

Never a tremor of wind, or a splash of rain, no
errant snowflake comes to stain that heaven, so
calm, so vaporless, the world of light.

—HOMER

One Equal

Bring us, O Lord God, at our last awakening, into
the house and gate of heaven, to enter into that gate
and dwell in that house where there shall be no
darkness nor dazzling, but one equal light; no noise
nor silence, but one equal music; no fears nor
hopes, but one equal possession; no ends nor
beginnings, but one equal eternity; in the habita-
tions of Thy glory and dominion, world without
end. Amen.

—JOHN ĐONNE

Harps

There is no need to be worried by facetious people
who try to make the Christian hope of "heaven"

ridiculous by saying they do not want "to spend eternity playing harps." The answer to such people is that if they cannot understand books written for grown-ups, they should not talk about them. All the scriptural imagery (harps, crowns, gold, etc.) is, of course, a merely symbolic attempt to express the inexpressible. Musical instruments are mentioned because for many people (not all) music is the thing known in the present life which most strongly suggests ecstasy and infinity. Crowns are mentioned to suggest the fact that those who are united with God in eternity share His splendour and power and joy. Gold is mentioned to suggest the timelessness of Heaven (gold does not rust) and the preciousness of it. People who take these symbols literally might as well think that when Christ told us to be like doves, He meant that we were to lay eggs.

——C. S. LEWIS

Behind the Scenes

DON JUAN: If the play still goes on here and on earth, and all the world is a stage, Heaven is at least behind the scenes.

——GEORGE BERNARD SHAW
(from *Man and Superman*)

Mother Country

Oh what is that country
And where can it be,

Not mine own country,
    But dearer far to me?
Yet mine own country,
    If I one day may see
Its spices and cedars,
    Its gold and ivory.

As I lie dreaming
    It rises, that land:
There rises before me
    Its green golden strand,
With its bowing cedars
    And its shining sand;
It sparkles and flashes
    Like a shaken brand.

Do angels lean nearer
    While I lie and long?
I see their soft plumage
    And watch their windy song,
Like the rise of a high tide
    Sweeping full and strong;
I mark the outskirts
    Of their reverend throng.

Oh what is a king here,
    Or what is a boor?
Here all starve together,
    All dwarfed and poor;

Here Death's hand knocketh
    At door after door,
He thins the dancers
    From the festal floor.

Oh, what is a handmaid,
    Or what is a queen?
All must lie down together
    Where the turf is green,
The foulest face hidden,
    The fairest not seen;
Gone as if never,
    They had breathed or been.

Gone from sweet sunshine
    Underneath the sod,
Turned from warm flesh and blood
    To senseless clod,
Gone as if never
    They had toiled or trod,
Gone out of sight of all
    Except our God.

Shut into silence
    From the accustomed song,
Shut into solitude
    From all earth's throng,
Run down tho' swift of foot,
    Thrust down tho' strong;
Life made an end of,
    Seemed it short or long.

Life made an end of,
    Life but just begun,
Life finished yesterday,
    Its last sand run;
Life new-born with the morrow,
    Fresh as the sun:

> While done is done for ever;
>> Undone, undone.
>
> And if that life is life,
>> This is but a breath,
> The passage of a dream
>> And the shadow of death;
> But a vain shadow
>> If one considereth;
> Vanity of vanities,
>> As the Preacher saith.

—CHRISTINA GEORGINA ROSSETTI

The Starlight Night

Look at the stars! look, look up at the skies!
O look at all the fire-folk sitting in the air!
The bright boroughs, the circle-citadels there!
Down in dim woods the diamond delves! the elves'-eyes!
The grey lawns cold where gold, where quickgold lies!
Wind-beat whitebeam! airy abeles set on a flare!
Flake-doves sent floating forth at a farmyard scare!—
Ah, well! it is all a purchase, all is a prize.

Buy then! bid then!—What?—Prayer, patience, alms, vows,
Look, look: a May-mess, like an orchard boughs!
Look! March-bloom, like on mealed-with-yellow sallows!
These are indeed the barn, within doors house
The shocks. This piece-bright paling shuts the spouse
Christ home, Christ and his mother and all his hallows.

—GERARD MANLEY HOPKINS

Age

"About how old might you be, Sandy?"

"Seventy-two."

"I judged so. How long you been in heaven?"

"Twenty-seven years, come Christmas."

"How old was you when you come up?"

"Why, seventy-two, of course."

"You can't mean it!"

"Why can't I mean it?"

"Because, if you was seventy-two then, you are naturally ninety-nine now."

"No, but I ain't. I stay the same age I was when I come."

"Well," says I, "come to think, there's something just here that I want to ask about. Down below, I always had an idea that in heaven we would all be young, and bright, and spry."

"Well, you can be young if you want to. You've only got to wish."

"Well, then, why didn't you wish?"

"I did. They all do. You'll try it, some day, like enough; but you'll get tired of the change pretty soon."

"Why?"

"Well, I'll tell you. Now you've always been a sailor; did you ever try some other business?"

"Yes, I tried keeping grocery, once, up in the mines; but I couldn't stand it; it was too dull—no stir, no storm, no life about it; it was like being part dead and part alive, both at the same time. I wanted to be one thing or t'other. I shut up shop pretty quick and went to sea."

"That's it. Grocery people like it, but you couldn't. You see you wasn't used to it. Well, I wasn't used to being young, and I couldn't seem to take any interest in it. I was strong, and handsome, and had curly hair,—yes, and wings, too!—gay wings like a butterfly. I went to picnics and dances and parties with the fellows, and tried to carry on and talk nonsense with the girls, but it wasn't any use; I couldn't take to it—fact is, it was an awful bore. What I wanted was early to bed and early to rise, and something to do; and when my work was done, I wanted to sit quiet, and smoke and think— not tear around with a parcel of giddy young kids. You can't think what I suffered whilst I was young."

"How long was you young?"

"Only two weeks. That was plenty for me. Laws, I was so lonesome! You see, I was full of the knowledge and experience of seventy-two years; the deepest subject those young folks could strike was only a-b-c to me. And to hear them argue— oh, my! it would have been funny, if it hadn't been so pitiful. Well, I was so hungry for the ways and the sober talk I was used to, that I tried to ring in with the old people, but they wouldn't have it. They considered me a conceited young upstart, and gave me the cold shoulder. Two weeks was a- plenty for me. I was glad to get back my bald head again, and my pipe, and my old drowsy reflections in the shade of a rock or a tree."

—MARK TWAIN
(from *Captain Stormfield's Visit to Heaven*)

I Heard Immanuel Singing

The poem shows the Master with work done, singing
to free His heart in Heaven.

I heard Immanuel singing   *(To be sung.)*
Within his own good lands;
I saw him bend above his harp.
I watched his wandering hands
Lost amid the harp-strings;
Sweet, sweet I heard him play.
His wounds were altogether healed.
Old things had passed away.

All things were new, but music.
The blood of David ran
Within the Son of David,
Our God, the Son of Man.
He was ruddy like a shepherd.
His bold young face, how fair.
Apollo of the silver bow
Had not such flowing hair.

I saw Immanuel singing   *(To be read very softly*
On a tree-girdled hill.   *but in spirited response.)*
The glad remembering branches
Dimly echoed still
The grand new song proclaiming
The Lamb that had been slain.
New-built, the Holy City
Gleamed in the murmuring plain.
The crowning hours were over.
The pageants all were past.

Within the many mansions
The hosts, grown still at last,
In homes of holy mystery
Slept long by crooning springs
Or waked to peaceful glory,
A universe of Kings.

He left his people happy.   *(To be sung.)*
He wandered free to sigh
Alone in lowly friendship
With the green grass and the sky.
He murmured ancient music
His red heart burned to sing
Because his perfect conquest
Had grown a weary thing.

No chant of gilded triumph—
His lonely song was made
Of Art's deliberate freedom;
Of minor chords arrayed
In soft and shadowy colors
That once were radiant flowers:—
The Rose of Sharon, bleeding
In Olive-shadowed bowers:—

And all the other roses
In the songs of East and West
Of love and war and worshipping,
And every shield and crest
Of thistle or of lotus
Or sacred lily wrought
In creeds and psalms and palaces
And temples of white thought:—

All these he sang, half-smiling   *(To be read very softly,*
And weeping as he smiled,   *yet in spirited response.)*
Laughing, talking to his harp
As to a new-born child:—
As though the arts forgotten
But bloomed to prophecy
These careless, fearless harp-strings,
New-crying in the sky.

"When this his hour of sorrow   *(To be sung.)*
For flowers and Arts of men
Has passed in ghostly music,"
I asked my wild heart then—
What will he sing tomorrow,
What wonder, all his own
Alone, set free, rejoicing
With a green hill for his throne?
What will he sing tomorrow,
What wonder all his own
Alone, set free, rejoicing,
With a green hill for his throne?

—VACHEL LINDSAY

The Chambered Nautilus

This is the ship of pearl which, poets feign,
     Sails the unshadowed main,—
     The venturous bark that flings
On the sweet summer wind its purpled wings
In gulfs enchanted, where the Siren sings,
     And coral reefs lie bare,
Where the cold sea-maids rise to sun their streaming hair.

Its webs of living gauze no more unfurl;
    Wrecked is the ship of pearl!
    And every chambered cell,
Where its dim dreaming life was wont to dwell,
As the frail tenant shaped his growing shell,
    Before thee lies revealed,—
Its irised ceiling rent, its sunless crypt unsealed!

Year after year beheld the silent toil
    That spread his lustrous coil;
    Still, as the spiral grew,
He left the past year's dwelling for the new,
Stole with soft step its shining archway through,
    Built up its idle door,
Stretched in his last-found home, and knew the old no
    more.

Thanks for the heavenly message brought by thee,
    Child of the wandering sea,
    Cast from her lap, forlorn!
From thy dead lips a clearer note is born
Than ever Triton blew from wreathed horn!
    While on mine ear it rings,
Through the deep caves of thought I hear a voice that
    sings:—

Build thee more stately mansions, O my soul,
    As the swift seasons roll!
    Leave thy low-vaulted past!
Let each new temple, nobler than the last,
Shut thee from heaven with a dome more vast,
    Till thou at length art free,
Leaving thine outgrown shell by life's unresting sea!

—OLIVER WENDELL HOLMES

Etiquette for the Afterlife

- Upon arrival in heaven do not speak to St. Peter until spoken to. It is not your place to begin.

- Wait patiently in the queue till it comes your turn to apply for a ticket. Do not look bored, and don't scratch your shin with your other foot.

- When applying for a ticket, avoid trying to make conversation. St. Peter is hard-worked and has no time for conversation. If you *must* talk, let the weather alone. St. Peter cares not a damn for the weather. And don't ask him what time the 4:30 train goes; there aren't any trains in heaven, except the through-trains for the other place, and the less information you get about them, the better for you.

- Don't tell him you used to have an uncle named after him, "maybe you have met him." He is tired of that.

- You can ask for his autograph—there is no harm in that—but be careful and don't remark that it is one of the penalties of greatness. He has heard that before.

- Do not try to show off. St. Peter dislikes it. The simpler you are dressed, the better it will please him. He cannot abide showy costumes. Above all things, avoid *over*-dressing. A pair of spurs and a fig-leaf is plenty.

- If you get in—if you get in—don't tip him. That is, publicly. Don't hand it to him, just leave a quarter on the bench by him, and let on you forgot it. If he bites it to see if it is good, you are not to seem to notice it.

- Leave your dog outside. Heaven goes by favor. If it went by merit, you would stay out and the dog would go in.

- Keep off the grass.

—MARK TWAIN

CHAPTER 2
"GOD GROWS ABOVE"

Where is Heaven? According to Henry Vaughan, it is a country "far beyond the stars." The tomb, says Victor Hugo, is but a "thoroughfare [that] closes upon the twilight but opens on the dawn." We read of Heaven located up in the sky or across the sea. Our stay on earth is all about the pilgrimage, the voyage, the journey to Emily Dickinson's God who "grows above."

Uphill

Does the road wind uphill all the way?
Yes, to the very end.
Will the day's journey take the whole long day?
From morn to night, my friend.

But is there for the night a resting place?
A roof for when the slow dark hours begin.
May not the darkness hide it from my face?
You cannot miss that inn.

Shall I meet other wayfarers at night?
Those who have gone before.
Then must I knock, or call when just in sight?
They will not keep you waiting at that door.

Shall I find comfort, travel-sore and weak?
Of labour you shall find the sum.
Will there be beds for me and all who seek?
Yea, beds for all who come.

—CHRISTINA GEORGINA ROSSETTI

Lost in Heaven

The clouds, the source of rain, one stormy night
Offered an opening to the source of dew;
Which I accepted with impatient sight,
Looking for my old skymarks in the blue.

But stars were scarce in that part of the sky,
And no two were of the same constellation—
No one was bright enough to identify;
So 'twas with not ungrateful consternation,

Seeing myself well lost once more, I sighed,
"Where, where in Heaven am I? But don't tell me!
Oh, opening clouds, by opening on me wide.
Let's let my heavenly lostness overwhelm me."

—ROBERT FROST

They Are All Gone into
the World of Light

They are all gone into the world of light!
    And I alone sit ling'ring here;
Their very memory is fair and bright,
    And my sad thoughts doth clear.

It glows and glitters in my cloudy breast
    Like stars upon some gloomy grove,
Or those faint beams in which this hill is dress'd,
    After the sun's remove.

I see them walking in an air of glory,
　　Whose light doth trample on my days:
My days, which are at best but dull and hoary,
　　Mere glimmering and decays.

O holy hope! and high humility,
　　High as the Heavens above!
These are your walks, and you have show'd them me
　　To kindle my cold love,

Dear, beauteous death! the Jewel of the Just,
　　Shining nowhere, but in the dark;
What mysteries do lie beyond thy dust;
　　Could man outlook that mark!

He that hath found some fledg'd bird's nest, may know
　　At first sight, if the bird be flown;
But what fair well, or grove he sings in now,
　　That is to him unknown.

And yet, as angels in some brighter dreams
　　Call to the soul, when man doth sleep:
So some strange thoughts transcend our wonted themes,
　　And into glory peep.

If a star were confin'd into a tomb
　　Her captive flames must needs burn there;
But when the hand that lock'd her up, gives room,
　　She'll shine through all the sphere.

O Father of eternal life, and all
　　Created glories under thee!
Resume thy spirit from this world of thrall
　　Into true liberty.

Either disperse these mists, which blot and fill
   My perspective (still) as they pass,
Or else remove me hence unto that hill,
   Where I shall need no glass.

—HENRY VAUGHAN

Peace

My soul, there is a country
   Far beyond the stars,
Where stands a winged sentry
   All skilful in the wars:
There, above noise and danger,
   Sweet Peace sits crowned with smiles,
And one born in a manger
   Commands the beauteous files.
He is thy gracious Friend,
   And—O my soul, awake!—
Did in pure love descend
   To die here for thy sake.
If thou canst get but thither,
   There grows the flower of Peace,
The Rose that cannot whither,
   Thy fortress and thy ease.
Leave then thy foolish ranges;
   For none can thee secure
But one who never changes—
   Thy God, thy life, thy cure.

—HENRY VAUGHAN

My Pilgrimage

Give me my scallop-shell of quiet,
My staff of faith to walk upon,
My scrip of joy, immortal diet,
My bottle of salvation,
My gown of glory, hope's true gage;
And thus I'll take my pilgrimage!

Blood must be my body's balmer;
No other balm will there be given,
Whilst my soul, like quiet palmer,
Travelleth toward the land of heaven,
Over the silver mountains,

Where spring the nectar fountains,
    There will I kiss
    The bowl of bliss;
And drink mine everlasting fill
Upon every milken hill
My soul will be a-dry before;
But, after, it will thirst no more.

Then by that happy, blissful day,
More peaceful pilgrims I shall see,
That have cast off their rags of clay,
And walk apparelled fresh like me.
    I'll take them first,
    To quench their thirst
And taste of nectar's suckets,
    At those clear wells
    Where sweetness dwells,
Drawn up by saints in crystal buckets.

And when our bottles and all we
Are filled with immortality,
Then the blessed paths we'll travel,
Strewed with rubies thick as gravel;
Ceilings of diamonds, sapphire floors,
High walls of coral, and pearly bowers.

From thence to heaven's bribeless hall,
Where no corrupted voices brawl;
No conscience molten into gold;
No forged accuser bought or sold;
No cause deferred, no vain-spent journey,
For there Christ is the King's Attorney,
Who pleads for all, without degrees,
And he hath angels but no fees.
And when the grand twelve-million jury
Of our sins, with direful fury,
Against our souls black verdicts give,
Christ pleads his death; and then we live.

Be thou my speaker, taintless Pleader!
Unblotted Lawyer! true Proceeder!
Thou giv'st salvation, even for alms,
Not with a bribed lawyer's palms.
And this is mine eternal plea
To Him that made heaven, earth and sea;
That, since my flesh must die so soon,
And want a head to dine next noon,—
Just at the stroke, when my veins start and spread,
Set on my soul an everlasting head!
Then I am ready, like a palmer fit,
To tread those blest paths; which before I writ.

O death and judgment, heaven and hell,
Who oft doth think, must needs die well.

—SIR WALTER RALEIGH

※

That Future Life

I feel within me that future life. I am like a forest
that has been razed; the new shoots are stronger
and brighter. I shall most certainly rise toward the
heavens . . . the nearer my approach to the end, the
plainer is the sound of immortal symphonies of
worlds which invite me. For half a century I have
been translating my thoughts into prose and verse:
history, philosophy, drama, romance, tradition,
satire, ode, and song; all of these I have tried. But I
feel I haven't given utterance to the thousandth
part of what lies with me. When I go to the grave I
can say, as others have said, "My day's work is
done." But I cannot say, "My life is done." My work
will recommence the next morning. The tomb is
not a blind alley; it is a thoroughfare. It closes upon
the twilight but opens upon the dawn.

—VICTOR HUGO

※

The Imprisoned Soul

At the last, tenderly
From the walls of the powerful fortressed house,
From the clasp of the knitted locks—
    from the keep of the well-closed doors,

Let me be wafted.

Let me glide noiselessly forth;
With the key of softness unlock the locks—
    with a whisper
Set ope the doors, O soul!

Tenderly! be not impatient!
(Strong is your hold, O mortal flesh!
Strong is your hold, O Love!)

—WALT WHITMAN

Rubáiyát of Omar Khayyám

Oh threats of Hell and Hopes of Paradise!
One thing at least is certain—This Life flies;
    One thing is certain and the rest is Lies;
The Flower that once has blown forever dies.

Strange, is it not? that of the myriads who
Before us pass'd the door of Darkness through,
    Not one returns to tell us of the Road,
Which to discover we must travel too.

The Revelations of Devout and Learn'd
Who rose before us, and as Prophets burn'd,
    Are all but Stories, which, awoke from Sleep,
They told their comrades, and to Sleep return'd.

I sent my Soul through the Invisible,
Some letter of that after-life to spell:
    And by and by my Soul return'd to me,
And answer'd "I Myself am Heav'n and Hell."

Heav'n but the Vision of fulfill'd Desire,
And Hell the Shadow from a Soul on fire,
 Cast on the Darkness into which Ourselves,
So late emerged from, shall so soon expire.

——TRANS. BY EDWARD FITZGERALD

Darest Thou Now, O Soul?

Darest thou now, O Soul,
Walk out with me toward the Unknown Region,
Where neither ground is for the feet, nor any path to
 follow?

No map, there, nor guide,
Nor voice sounding, nor touch of human hand,
Nor face with blooming flesh, nor lips, nor eyes, are
 in that land.

I know it not, O Soul;
Nor dost thou, all is a blank before us,—
All waits, undreamed of, in that region—
 that inaccessible land.

Till, when the tie is loosened,
All but the ties eternal, Time and Space,
Nor darkness, gravitation, sense, nor any bounds
 bound us.

Then we burst forth, we float,
In Time and Space, O Soul! prepared for them;
Equal, equipped at last (O joy! O fruit of all!) them
 to fulfill, O Soul!

——WALT WHITMAN

God Grows Above

God grows above—so those who pray
Horizons—must ascend—
And so I stepped upon the North
To see this Curious Friend—

His House was not—no sign had He—
By Chimney—nor by Door
Could I infer his Residence—
Vast Prairies of Air

Unbroken by a Settler—
Were all that I could see—
Infinitude—Had'st Thou no Face
That I might look on Thee?

The Silence condescended—
Creation stopped—for Me—
But awed beyond my errand—
I worshipped—did not "pray"—

—EMILY DICKINSON

Song of the Silent Land

Into the Silent Land!
Ah! who shall lead us thither?
Clouds in the evening sky more darkly gather,
And shattered wrecks lie thicker on the strand,
Who leads us with a gentle hand
Thither, oh, thither,
Into the Silent Land?

Into the Silent Land!
To you, ye boundless regions
Of all perfection! Tender morning-visions
Of beauteous souls! The Future's pledge and band
Who in Life's battle firm doth stand,
Shall bear Hope's tender blossoms
Into the Silent Land!

O Land! O Land!
For all the broken-hearted
The mildest herald by our fate allotted,
Beckons, and with inverted torch doth stand
To lead us with a gentle hand
To the land of the great Departed,
Into the Silent Land!

——HENRY WADSWORTH LONGFELLOW

Heavenly Jerusalem

"There," said they, "is the Mount Sion, the heavenly Jerusalem, the innumerable company of angels, and the spirits of just men made perfect. You are going now," said they, "to the Paradise of God, wherein you shall see the Tree of Life, and eat of the never-fading fruits thereof; and when you come there you shall have white robes given you, and your walk and talk shall be every day with the King, even all the days of eternity. There you shall not see again such things as you saw when you were in the lower region upon the earth, to wit, sorrow, sickness, affliction, and death, for the former things are passed away. . . ."

The men then asked, "What must we do in the holy place?" To whom it was answered, "You must there receive the comfort of all your toil, and have joy for all your sorrow; you must reap what you have sown, even the fruit of all your prayers and tears, and sufferings for the King by the way. In that place you must wear crowns of gold, and enjoy the perpetual sight and visions of the Holy One, for there you shall see him as he is. . . ."

There came out also at this time to meet them several of the King's trumpeters, clothed in white and shining raiment, who with melodious noises and loud, made even the Heavens to echo with their sound.

Now I saw in my dream, that these two men went in at the gate; and lo, as they entered, they were transfigured, and they had raiment put on that shone like gold. There was also that met them with harps and crowns, and gave to them; the harp to praise withal, and the crowns in token of honour. Then I heard in my dream that all the bells in the City rang again for joy, and that it was said unto them, "Enter ye into the joy of your Lord." I also heard the men themselves, that they sang with a loud voice, saying, "Blessing, honour, glory, and power, be to him that sitteth upon the throne, and to the Lamb forever and ever."

Now just as the gates were opened to let in the men, I looked in after them; and behold, the City shone like the sun, the streets also were paved with gold, and in them walked many men, with crowns on their heads, palms in their hands, and golden harps to sing praises withal. There were also of them that had wings, and they answered one another without intermission, saying, "Holy, Holy, Holy, is the Lord." And after that, they shut up the gates, which when I had seen, I wished myself among them.

—JOHN BUNYAN

The Dying Christian to His Soul

Vital spark of heavenly flame!
Quit, O quit this mortal frame!
Trembling, hoping, lingering, flying,
O the pain, the bliss of dying!
Cease, fond Nature, cease thy strife,
And let me languish into life!

Hark! they whisper; angels say—
"Sister Spirit, come away!"
What is this absorbs me quite?
Steals my senses, shuts my sight,
Drowns my spirit, draws my breath?
Tell me, my soul, can this be death?

The world recedes; it disappears!
Heaven opens on my eyes! my ears
With sounds seraphic ring!
Lend, lend your wings! I mount! I fly!
O Grave! where is thy victory?
O Death! where is thy sting?

—ALEXANDER POPE

The Two Ships

As I stand by the cross on the lone mountain's crest,
  Looking over the ultimate sea,
In the gloom of the mountain a ship lies at rest,
  And one sails away from the lea:
One spreads its white wings on a far-reaching track,
  With pennant and sheet flowing free;
One hides in the shadow with sails laid aback,—
The ship that is waiting for me!

But lo! in the distance the clouds break away,
  The Gate's glowing portals I see;
And I hear from the outgoing ship in the bay
  The song of the sailors in glee.
So I think of the luminous footprints that bore
  The comfort o'er dark Galilee,
And wait for the signal to go to the shore,
To the ship that is waiting for me.

—BRET HARTE

Older Than Eden

This world is wild as an old wives' tale,
And strange the plain things are,
The earth is enough and the air is enough
For our wonder and our war;
But our rest is as far as the fire-drake swings
And our peace is put in impossible things
Where clashed and thundered unthinkable wings
Round an incredible star.

To an open house in the evening
Home shall men come,
To an older place than Eden
And a taller town than Rome.
To the end of the way of the wandering star,
To the things that cannot be and that are,
To the place where God was homeless
And all men are at home.

—G. K. CHESTERTON

Passage to More Than India

O Thou transcendent!
Nameless—the fibre and the breath!
Light of the light—shedding forth universes—the
    centre of them!
Thou mightier centre of the true, the good, the loving!
Thou moral, spiritual fountain! affection's source!
    thou reservoir!
Thou pulse! thou motive of the stars, suns, systems,
That, circling, move in order, safe, harmonious,
Athwart the shapeless vastnesses of space!
How should I think—how breathe a single breath—
    how speak—if, out of myself,
I could not launch, to those, superior universes!

Passage to more than India!
Are thy wings plumed indeed for such far flights?
O Soul, voyagest thou indeed on voyages like these?
Disportest thou on waters such as these?
Soundest below the Sanscrit and the Vedas?
Then have thy bent unleashed.

Passage to you, your shores, ye aged fierce enigmas!
Passage to you, to mastership of you, ye strangling
   problems!
You, strewed with the wrecks of skeletons, that, living,
   never reached you.

Passage—immediate passage! the blood burns in my
   veins!
Away, O soul! hoist instantly the anchor!
Cut the hawsers—haul out—shake out every sail!
Have we not stood here like trees in the ground long
   enough?
Have we not grovelled here long enough, eating and
   drinking like mere brutes?
Have we not darkened and dazed ourselves with
   books long enough?

Sail forth! steer for the deep waters only!
Reckless, O soul, exploring, I with thee, and thou
   with me;
For we are bound where mariner has not yet dared
   to go,
And we will risk the ship, ourselves and all.

O my brave soul!
O farther, farther sail!
O daring joy, but safe! Are they not all the seas of God?
O farther, farther, farther sail.

—WALT WHITMAN
(from *Passage to India*)

Eternity

O years! and Age! Farewell:
   Behold I go,
   Where I do know
Infinity to dwell.

And these mine eyes shall see
   All times, how they
   Are lost i' th' Sea
Of vast Eternity.

Where never Moon shall sway
   The Stars; but she,
   And Night, shall be
Drown'd in one endless Day.

—ROBERT HERRICK

Heaven

Fish (fly-replete, in depth of June,
Daw'dling away their wat'ry noon)
Ponder deep wisdom, dark or clear,
Each secret fishy hope or fear.
Fish say, they have their Stream and Pond;
But is there anything Beyond?
This life cannot be All, they swear,
For how unpleasant, if it were!
One may not doubt that, somehow, Good
Shall come of Water and of Mud;
And, sure, the reverent eye must see
A Purpose in Liquidity.
We darkly know, by Faith we cry,

The future is not Wholly Dry.
Mud unto mud!—Death eddies near—
Not here the appointed End, not here!
But somewhere, beyond Space and Time.
Is wetter water, slimier slime!
And there (they trust) where swimmeth One
Who swam ere rivers were begun,
Immense, of fishy form and mind,
Squamous, omnipotent, and kind;
And under that Almighty Fin,
The littlest fish may enter in,
Oh! never fly conceals a hook,
Fish say, in the Eternal Brook,
But more than mundane weeds are there,
And mud, celestially fair;
Fat caterpillars drift around,
And Paradisal grubs are found;
Unfading moths, immortal flies,
And the worm that never dies.
And in that Heaven of all their wish,
There shall be no more land, say fish.

—RUPERT BROOKE

CHAPTER 3
"JOY IS THE SERIOUS BUSINESS OF HEAVEN"

John Keats suggested a Heaven filled "with superior bliss" that is a "region of peace and everlasting love." Many great writers across the centuries have agreed with him. More than an earthly perfection, this conception of Heaven embraces the soul, the spirit, intellectual and emotional fulfillment, even ecstasy. D. H. Lawrence described Heaven as a "Holy of Holies" where the "silent soul may sink into god at last."

As from the Darkening Gloom
(written upon the death of Keats's grandmother)

As from the darkening gloom a silver dove
Upsoars, and darts into the Eastern light,
On pinions that naught moves but pure delight,
So fled thy soul into the realms above,
Region of peace and everlasting love;
Where happy spirits, crown'd with circlets bright
Of starry beam, and gloriously bedight,
Taste the high joy none but the blest can prove.
There thou or joinest the immortal quire
In melodies that even Heaven fair
Fill with superior bliss, or, at desire
Of the omnipotent Father, cleavest the air
On holy message sent—What pleasure's higher
Wherefore does any grief our joy impair?

—JOHN KEATS

Tabernacle

Come, let us build a temple to oblivion
with seven veils, and an innermost
Holy of Holies of sheer oblivion.

And there oblivion dwells, and the silent soul
may sink into god at last, having passed the veils.

But anyone who shall ascribe attributes to God or
   oblivion
let him be cast out, for blasphemy.
For God is a deeper forgetting far than sleep
and all description is a blasphemy.

—D. H. LAWRENCE

The Choir Invisible

Oh, may I join the choir invisible
Of those immortal dead who live again
In minds made better by their presence; live
In pulses stirred to generosity,
In deeds of daring rectitude, in scorn
For miserable aims that end with self,
In thought sublime that pierce the night like stars,
And with their mild persistence urge men's search
To vaster issues. So to live is heaven:
To make undying music in the world,
Breathing a beauteous order that controls
With growing sway the growing life of man.

This is life to come,—
Which martyred men have made more glorious
For us who strive to follow. May I reach
That purest heaven,—be to other souls
The cup of strength in some great agony,
Enkindle generous ardor, feed pure love,
Beget the smiles that have no cruelty—
Be the sweet presence of a good diffused,
And in diffusion even more intense.
So shall I join the choir invisible
Whose music is the gladness of the world.

—GEORGE ELIOT

No Coward Soul Is Mine

No coward soul is mine
No trembler in the world's storm-troubled sphere
I see Heaven's glories shine
And Faith stands equal arming me from Fear

O God within my breast
Almighty ever-present Deity
Life, that in me has rest
As I Undying Life, have power in Thee

Though Earth and moon were gone
And suns and universes ceased to be
And thou wert left alone
Every Existence would exist in thee

There is not room for Death
Nor atom that his might could render void

Since thou art Being and Breath
And what thou art may never be destroyed.

—EMILY BRONTË

Divine Compassion

Long since, a dream of heaven I had,
    And still the vision haunts me oft;
I see the saints in white robes clad,
    The martyrs with their palms aloft;
But hearing still, in middle song,
    The ceaseless dissonance of wrong;
And shrinking, with hid faces, from the strain
Of sad, beseeching eyes, full of remorse and pain.

The glad song falters to a wail,
    The harping sinks to low lament;
Before the still unlifted veil
    I see the crowned foreheads bent,
Making more sweet the heavenly air
    With breathings of unselfish prayer;
And a Voice saith: "O Pity which is pain,
O love that weeps, fill up my sufferings which
    remain!

"Shall souls redeemed by me refuse
    To share my sorrow in their turn?
Or, sin-forgiven, my gift abuse
    Of peace with selfish unconcern?
Has saintly ease no pitying care?
    Has faith no work, and love no prayer?
While sin remains, and souls in darkness dwell,
Can heaven itself be heaven, and look unmoved on hell?"

Then through the Gates of Pain, I dream,
    A wind of heaven blows cooly in;
Fainter the awful discords seem,
    The smoke of torment grows more thin,
Tears quench the burning soil, and thence
    Spring sweet, pale flowers of penitence:
And through the dreary realm of man's despair,
Star-crowned an angel walks, and Lo! God's hope is
    there!

Is it a dream? Is heaven so high
    That pity cannot breathe its air?
Its happy eyes forever dry,
    Its holy lips without a prayer!
My God! My God! if thither led
    By Thy free grace unmerited,
No crown nor palm be mine, but let me keep
A heart that still can feel, and eyes that still can weep.

—JOHN GREENLEAF WHITTIER

A Spirit Appeared to Me

A spirit appeared to me, and said
"Where now would you choose to dwell?
In the Paradise of the Fool,
Or in wise Solomon's hell?"

Never he asked me twice:
"Give me the Fool's Paradise."

—HERMAN MELVILLE

I Reason

I reason, earth is short,
And anguish absolute.
And many hurt;
But what of that?

I reason, we could die:
The best vitality
Cannot excel decay;
But what of that?

I reason that in heaven
Somehow, it will be even,
Some new equation given;
But what of that?

—EMILY DICKINSON

If Tolling Bell

If tolling bell I ask the cause.
"A soul has gone to God,"
I'm answered in a lonesome tone;
Is heaven then so sad?

That bells should joyful ring to tell
A soul had gone to heaven,
Would seem to me the proper way
A good news should be given.

—EMILY DICKINSON

Miriam's Miracle

A painter of the Middle Ages, depicting lost souls being herded into Hell after the Last Judgment, would not have made use of those hideous drab surroundings, nor would he have included children among the damned, nor would he have clothed the devils in black nor armed them with whips and pistols. Nor would he have thought to include among the damned a young woman with a harelip.

Miriam went along with the others. Somehow, incredibly, she still had hope. She was still praying for a miracle. It still did not seem impossible to her that there should be one. Like the others, she looked up at the threatening autumn sky. If there was no sign of hope there as yet there still might be one. Then this awful procession would end, and then these pitiful victims would tread triumphant over the prostrate bodies of their tormentors.

But the miracle was long in coming. The head of the procession reached the door of the building. Here there was dreadful fear, and the leaders hung back pitifully, as the guards round the door made them deposit their clothes in a pile and then go in over the threshold. Blows and threats were necessary here. In the slaughterhouses of Chicago they have a Judas goat to lead the sheep to the butcher; he goes free each time and apparently enjoys his work, but Schiller had not been ingenious enough to think of some similar device. The first among his victims had to be kicked and shoved with violence in through the door; and the others were driven in after them, pushing the leaders towards the far end of the building although they did not want to go there, but wanted to stay near the entrance. Slowly the crowd was driven in, old men and old women and children, the cripples and the diseased, more and more and more of them, packed tight. Miriam was in the center, with naked flesh pressed close against her naked flesh, but she was no more conscious of it than were the others. This would be the time; this would be the moment. Then the door was slammed shut, and the windowless building lost its faint light and became pitch dark inside; the instant coming of darkness was marked by a climax in the screaming within the building, and Schiller outside gave an order to the member of the Extermination Squad who stood by the machine.

That was when Miriam had her miracle. The screaming around her stopped, and the roof was torn wide open to reveal blue skies and streaming sunshine—sunshine so bright that momentarily it hurt her eyes. But only momentarily; she was in bliss. The people around her were laughing with the joy of it. The world had changed, and the horror and bestiality had vanished. When she put her hand to her face she was not surprised—although the absence of surprise did not diminish her joy— to find that her harelip was healed and she was as beautiful as the day.

—C. S. FORESTER

The Chimney Sweeper

And by came an Angel who had a bright key,
And he open'd the coffins & set them all free.
Then down a green plain leaping laughing they run
And wash in a river and shine in the Sun.

—WILLIAM BLAKE

Joy Arises

I arise out of the dewy night and shake my wings.

Tears and lamentations are no more. Life and
death lie stretched below me. I breathe the sweet
aether blowing of the breath of God.

Deep as the universe is my life—and I know it;
nothing can dislodge the knowledge of it; nothing can
destroy, nothing can harm me.

Joy, joy arises—I arise. The sun darts overpower-
ing piercing rays of joy through me, the night radiates
it from me.

I take wings through the night and pass through
all the wilderness of the worlds, and the old dark
holds of tears and death—and return with laughter,
laughter, laughter:

Sailing through the starlit spaces on outspread
wings, we two—O laughter! laughter! laughter!

—EDWARD CARPENTER

A Hymn to Saint Teresa

How kindly will thy gentle heart
Kiss the sweetly-killing dart,
And close in his embraces keep
Those delicious wounds, that weep
Balsam to heal themselves with; thus
When these thy deaths, so numerous
Shall all at last die into one,
And melt thy soul's sweet mansion;
Like a soft lump of incense, hasted
By too hot a fire, and wasted
Into perfuming cloud, so fast
Shalt thou exhale to Heaven at last
In a resolving sigh, and then
O what? Ask not the tongues of men;
Angels cannot tell; suffice
Thyself shalt feel thine own joys,
And hold them fast for ever there,

So soon as thou shalt first appear.
The moon of maiden stars, thy white
Mistress, attended by such bright
Souls as thy shining self, shall come,
And in her first ranks make thee room;
Where 'mongst her snowy family
Immortal welcomes wait for thee.

O what delight, when revealed Life shall stand,
And teach thy lips Heaven with His hand;
On which thou now may'st to thy wishes
Heap up thy consecrated kisses.

What joys shall seize thy soul, when she,
Bending her blessed eyes on Thee,

   (Those second smiles of Heaven,) shall dart
Her mild rays through Thy melting heart.

   Angels, thy old friends, there shall greet thee,
Glad at their own home now to meet thee.

   All thy good works which went before
And waited for thee, at the door,
Shall own thee there; and all in one
Weave a constellation
Of crowns, with which the King thy Spouse
Shall build up thy triumphant brows.

   All thy old woes shall now smile on thee,
And thy pains sit bright upon thee,

   (All thy sorrows here shall shine,)
All thy sufferings be divine:
Tears shall take comfort, and turn gems,
And wrongs repent to diadems.
Even thy deaths shall live; and new—
Dress the soul, that erst they slew.
Thy wounds shall blush to such bright scars
As keep account of the Lamb's wars.

   Thou shalt look round bout, and see
Thousands of crown'd souls throng to be
Themselves thy crown: sons of thy vows.
The virgin-birth with which thy sovereign Spouse
Made fruitful thy fair soul. Go now
And with them all about thee, bow
To Him; put on, (He'll say,) put on

   (My rosy love) that thy rich zone
Sparkling with the sacred flames
Of thousand souls, with whose happy names

Heaven keep upon thy score; (Thy bright
Life brought them first to kiss the light,
That kindled them to stars,) and so
Thou with the Lamb, thy Lord shalt go,
And whereso'er He sets His white
Steps, walk with Him those ways of light
Which who in death would live to see,
Must learn in life to die like thee.

—RICHARD CRASHAW

Heaven-Haven

I have desired to go
    Where springs not fail,
To fields where flies no sharp and sided hail,
    And a few lilies blow.

And I have asked to be
    Where no storms come,
Where the green swell is in the havens dumb,
    And out of the swing of the sea.

—GERARD MANLEY HOPKINS

Favour of God

Finding him in a very good humour, I ventured to
lead him to the subject of our situation in a future
state, having much curiosity to know his notions
on that point. Samuel Johnson: "Why, Sir, the happiness of an unembodied spirit will consist in a
consciousness of the favour of God, in the con-

templation of truth, and in the possession of felici-
tating ideas."

—JAMES BOSWELL
(from the *Life of Johnson*)

Understandings

Men are admitted into heaven not because they
have curbed and governed their passions or have no
passions but because they have cultivated their
understandings. The treasures of heaven are not
negations of passion but realities of intellect from
which all the passions emanate uncurbed in their
eternal glory. The fool shall not enter into heaven
let him be ever so holy. Holiness is not the price of
entrance into heaven. Those who are cast out are all
those who, having no passions of their own because
of no intellect, have spent their lives in curbing and
governing other people's by the various arts of
poverty and cruelty of all kinds.

—WILLIAM BLAKE

Son of God, Son of Glory

I shall rise from the dead, from the prostration of
death, and never miss the sun, which shall be put
out, for I shall see the Son of God, the Sun of
Glory, and shine myself as that sun shines. I shall
rise from the grave, and never miss this city, which
shall be nowhere, for I shall see the city of God, the
new Jerusalem. I shall look up and never wonder

when it shall be day, for the angel will tell me that time shall be no more, and I shall see and see cheerfully that last day of judgment, which shall have no night, never end, and be united to the Ancient of Days, to God Himself, who had no morning, never began.

—JOHN DONNE

Now there are some things we all know, but we don't take'm out and look at'm very often. We all know that something is eternal. And it ain't houses and it ain't names, and it ain't earth, and it ain't even the stars . . . everybody knows in their bones that something is eternal, and that something has to do with human beings. All the greatest people ever lived have been telling us that for five thousand years and yet you'd be surprised how people are always losing hold of it. There's something way down deep that's eternal about every human being.

You know as well as I do that the dead don't stay interested in us living people for very long. Gradually, gradually, they lose hold of the earth . . . and the ambitions they had . . . and the pleasures they had . . . and the things they suffered . . . and the people they loved.

They get weaned away from earth—that's the way I put it,—weaned away.

And they stay here while the earth part of 'em burns away, burns out; and all that time they slowly get indifferent to what's goin' on in Grover's Corners.

They're waitin'. They're waitin' for something that they feel is comin'. Something important, and great. Aren't they waitin' for the eternal part in them to come out clear? Some of the things they're going to say maybe'll hurt your feelings—but that's the way it is: mother 'n daughter . . . husband 'n wife . . . enemy 'n enemy . . . money 'n miser . . . all those terribly important things kind of grow pale around here. And what's left when memory's gone, and your identity?

—THORNTON WILDER
(from *Our Town*)

Eden of God

The Eden of God is bare and grand: like the outdoor landscape remembered from the evening fireside, it seems cold and desolate whilst you cower over coals, but once abroad again, we pity those who can forego the magnificence of nature for candle-light and cards. . . . For God is the bride or bridegroom of the soul. Heaven is not the pairing of two, but the communion of all souls. We meet, and dwell an instant under the temple of one thought, and part, as though we parted not, to join another thought in other fellowships of joy. So far from there being anything divine in the low and proprietary sense of "Do you love me?" it is only when you leave and lose me by casting yourself on a sentiment which is higher than both of us, that I draw near and find myself at your side; and I am repelled if you fix your eye on me and demand love. In fact, in the spiritual world we change sexes every moment. You love the worth in me; then I am your husband: but it is not me, but the worth, that fixes the love; and that worth is a drop of the ocean of worth that is beyond me. Meantime I adore the greater worth in another, and so become his wife. He aspires to a higher worth in another spirit, and is wife or receiver of that influence.

—RALPH WALDO EMERSON

Joys of Heaven

Howling is the noise of Hell, singing the voice of Heaven; sadness the damp of Hell, rejoicing the serenity of Heaven. He that has not this joy here lacks one of the best pieces of evidence for the joys of Heaven, and has neglected or refused that earnest which God uses to bind his bargain, that true joy in this world shall flow into the joy of Heaven, as a river flows into the sea. This joy shall not be put out in death and a new joy kindled in me in Heaven; but as my soul, as soon as it is out of my body, is in Heaven, so the true joy of a good soul in this world is the very joy of Heaven.

—JOHN DONNE

Harmony

From harmony, from heavenly harmony
    This universal frame began;
   When Nature underneath a heap
    Of jarring atoms lay,
  And could not heave her head,
The tuneful voice was heard from high,
    "Arise, ye more than dead!"

Then cold and hot and moist and dry
   In order to their stations leap,
    And Music's power obey.
From harmony, from heavenly harmony,
    This universal frame began:
    From harmony to harmony
Through all the compass of the notes it ran,
The diapason closing full in Man . . .

   But Oh! what art can teach,
   What human voice can reach
    The sacred organ's praise?
  Notes inspiring holy love,
Notes that wing their heavenly ways
   To mend the choirs above.

Orpheus could lead the savage race,
And trees uprooted left their place,
   Sequacious of the lyre;
But bright Cecilia raised the wonder higher:
When to her organ vocal breath was given.
An angel heard, and straight appeared,
   Mistaking Earth for Heaven.

            —JOHN DRYDEN
     (from *A Song for St. Cecilia's Day*)

The Messenger

A Messenger of Hope comes every night to me,
And offers for short life eternal liberty.
He comes with western winds, with evening's wandering
    airs,
With that clear dusk of heaven that brings the thickest
    stars;
Winds take a pensive tone and stars a tender fire,
And visions rise and change, that kill me with
    desire—
Desire for nothing known in my maturer years,
When Joy grew mad with awe at counting future
    tears;
When, if my spirit's sky was full of flashes warm,
I knew not whence they came—from sun or thunder
    storm.
But first, a hush of peace—a soundless calm—
    descends;
The struggle of distress and fierce impatience ends;
Mute music soothes my breast, unuttered harmony
That I could never dream till Earth was lost to me.
Then dawns the Invisible; the Unseen its truth reveals;
My outward sense is gone, my inward essence feels;
Its wings are almost free, its home, its harbour found,
Measuring the gulf, it stoops and dares the final
    bound.

—EMILY BRONTË
(from *The Prisoner*)

Joy: Heaven's "Serious Business"

I do not think that the life of Heaven bears any analogy to play or dance in respect of frivolity. I do think
that while we are in this "valley of tears," cursed
with labor, hemmed round with necessities,
tripped up with frustrations, doomed to perpetual
plannings, puzzlings, and anxieties, certain qualities
that must belong to the celestial condition have no
chance to get through, can project no image of
themselves, except in activities which, for us here
and now, are frivolous. For surely we must suppose
the life of the blessed to be an end in itself, indeed
The End: to be utterly spontaneous; to be the complete reconciliation of boundless freedom with
order—with the most delicately adjusted, supple,
intricate, and beautiful order. How can you find any
image of this in the "serious" activities either of our
natural or of our (present) spiritual life? . . . No . . .
It is only in our "hours off," only in our hours of per-
mitted festivity, that we find an analogy. Dance and
game are frivolous, unimportant down here; for
"down here" is not their natural place. Here, they
are a moment's rest from the life we were placed
here to live. But in this world everything is upside
down. That which, if it could be prolonged here,
would be a truancy, is likest that which in a better
country is the End of Ends. Joy is the serious business of Heaven.

—C. S. LEWIS
(from *Letters to Malcolm: Chiefly on Prayer*)

I Took One Draught of Life

I took one Draught of Life—
I'll tell you what I paid—
Precisely an existence—
The market price, they said.

They weighed me, Dust by Dust—
They balanced Film with Film,
Then handed me my Being's worth—
A single Dram of Heaven!

—EMILY DICKINSON

CHAPTER 4
"ME IMMORTALIZED, AND YOU"

A wonderful thing about going to Heaven, Charles Dickens advised us, is that we are "all to meet each other after we are dead, and there be happy always together." He's not alone in yearning for those he loved on earth to be with him in eternity. Harriet Beecher Stowe looks forward to the "sweet hearts around us [that] throb and beat." And C. S. Lewis predicted that the "faces of our friends [will] laugh upon us with amazed recognition." Husbands and wives, lovers, brothers and sisters—all will be reunited in Heaven.

My Dear Children

My Dear Children, I am very anxious that you should know something about the History of Jesus Christ. For everybody ought to know about Him. No one ever lived, who was so good, so kind, so gentle, and so sorry for all people who did wrong, or were in any way ill or miserable, as he was. And as he is now in Heaven, where we hope to go, and all to meet each other after we are dead, and there be happy always together, you never can think what a good place Heaven is, without knowing who he was and what he did.

—CHARLES DICKENS

The White Island
or Place of the Blest

In this world, the Isle of Dreams,
While we sit by sorrow's streams,
Tears and terrors are our themes
    Reciting:

But when once from hence we fly,
More and more approaching nigh
Unto young Eternity
    Uniting:

In that whiter island, where
Things are evermore sincere;
Candor here and luster there
    Delighting:

There no monstrous fancies shall
Out of Hell an horror call,
To create (or cause at all)
    Affrighting.

There in calm and cooling sleep
We our eyes shall never steep;
But eternal watch shall keep
    Attending

Pleasures such as shall pursue
Me immortalized, and you;
And fresh joys, as never too
    Have ending.

—ROBERT HERRICK

The Other World

It lies around us like a cloud—
    The world we do not see;
Yet the sweet closing of an eye
    May bring us there to be.

Its gentle breezes fan our cheeks
    Amid our worldly cares;
Its gentle voices whisper love,
    And mingle with our prayers.

Sweet hearts around us throb and beat,
    Sweet helping hands are stirred,
And palpitates the veil between
    With breathings almost heard.

The silence—awful, sweet, and calm
    They have no power to break;
For mortal words are not for them
    To utter or partake.

So thin, so soft, so sweet they glide,
    So near to press they seem,
They lull us gently to our rest,
    And melt into our dream.

And, in the hush of rest they bring,
    'Tis easy now to see
How lovely and how sweet a pass
    The hour of death may be!

To close the eye and close the ear,
    Wrapped in a trance of bliss,
And, gently drawn in loving arms,
    To swoon to that—from this.

Scarce knowing if we wake or sleep,
　　Scarce asking where we are,
To feel all evil sink away,
　　All sorrow and all care.

Sweet souls around us! watch us still,
　　Press nearer to our side,
Into our thoughts, into our prayers,
　　With gentle helping glide.

Let death between us be as naught,
　　A dried and vanished stream;
Your joy be the reality,
　　Our suffering life the dream.

——HARRIET BEECHER STOWE

Sunshine of Eternal Bliss

To us, then, my friends, the promises of happiness
in heaven should be peculiarly dear, for if our
reward be in this life alone, we are indeed, of all
men the most miserable. When I look round these
gloomy walls, made to terrify, as well as to confine
us; this light, that only serves to show the horrors
of the place; those shackles, that tyranny has
imposed or crime made necessary; when I survey
these emaciated looks, and hear these groans:——
oh, my friends, what a glorious exchange would
heaven be for these! To fly through regions uncon-
fined as air——to bask in the sunshine of eternal
bliss——to carol over endless hymns or praise——to
have no master to threaten or insult us, but the

form of Goodness Himself for ever in our eyes:
when I think of these things, death becomes the
messenger of very glad tidings; when I think of
these things, his sharpest arrow becomes the staff
of my support; when I think of these things, what
is there in life worth having? when I think of these
things, what is there that should not be spurned
away? Kings in their palaces should groan for such
advantages; but we, humbled as we are, should
yearn for them. . . .

Then let us take comfort now, for we shall soon
be at our journey's end; we shall soon lay down the
heavy burden laid by Heaven upon us; and though
death, the only friend of the wretched, for a little
while mocks the weary traveller with the view,
and, like the horizon, still flies before him, yet the
time will certainly and shortly come when we shall
cease from our toil; when the luxurious great ones
of the world shall no more tread us to the earth;
when we shall think with pleasure of our sufferings
below; when we shall be surrounded with all our
friends, or such as deserved our friendship; when
our bliss shall be unutterable, and still, to crown
all, unending.

—OLIVER GOLDSMITH
(the Vicar's address to his companions in jail
from *The Vicar of Wakefield*)

The Flower to the Root

The hills and valleys of Heaven will be to those you
now experience not as a copy is to an original, nor

as a substitute is to the genuine article, but as the flower to the root, or the diamond to the coal. . . . Then the new earth and sky, the same yet not the same as these, will rise in us as we have risen in Christ. And once again, after who knows what aeons of the silence and the dark, the birds will sing and the waters flow, and lights and shadows move across the hills, and the faces of our friends laugh upon us with amazed recognition.

—C. S. LEWIS

The Blessed Damozel

The blessed damozel leaned out
    From the gold bar of heaven;
Her eyes were deeper than the depth
    Of waters stilled at even;
She had three lilies in her hand,
    And the stars in her hair were seven.

Her robe, ungirt from clasp to hem,
    No wrought flowers did adorn,
But a white rose of Mary's gift,
    For service meetly worn;
Her hair that lay along her back
    Was yellow like ripe corn.

Herseemed she scarce had been a day
    One of God's choristers;
The wonder was not yet quite gone
    From that still look of hers;

Albeit, to them she left, her day
    Had counted as ten years.

It was the rampart of God's house
    That she was standing on;
By God built over the sheer depth
    The which is Space begun;
So high, that looking downward thence
    She scarce could see the sun.

It lies in heaven, across the flood
    Of ether, as a bridge.
Beneath, the tides of day and night
    With flame and darkness ridge
The void, as low as where this earth
    Spins like a fretful midge.

Around her, lovers, newly met
    'Mid deathless love's acclaims
Spake evermore among themselves
    Their heart-remember'd names;
And the souls mounting up to God
    Went by her like thin flames.

And still she bowed herself and stooped
    Out of the circling charm;
Until her bosom must have made
    The bar she leaned on warm,
And the lilies lay as if asleep
    Along her bended arm.

From the fixed place of heaven she saw
    Time like a pulse shake fierce
Through all the worlds. Her gaze still strove
    Within the gulf to pierce

The path; and now she spoke as when
    The stars sang in their spheres.

The sun was gone now; the curled moon
    Was like a little feather
Fluttering far down the gulf; and now
    She spoke through the still weather.
Her voice was like the voice the stars
    Had when they sang together.

"I wish that he were come to me,
    For he will come," she said.
"Have I not prayed in heaven?—on earth,
    Lord, Lord, has he not prayed?
Are not two prayers a perfect strength!
    And shall I feel afraid?

"When round his head the aureole clings,
    And he is clothed in white,
I'll take his hand and go with him
    To the deep wells of light;
As unto a stream we will step down,
    And bathe there in God's sight.

"We two will stand beside that shrine,
    Occult, withheld, untrod,
Whose lamps are stirred continually
    With prayer sent up to God;
And see our old prayers, granted, melt
    Each like a little cloud.

"We two will lie i' the shadow of
    That living mystic tree,
Within whose secret growth the Dove
    Is sometimes felt to be,

While every leaf that His plumes touch
    Saith His Name audibly.

"And I myself will teach to him,
    I myself, lying so.
The songs I sing here; which his voice
    Shall pause in, hushed and slow,
And find some knowledge at each pause,
    Or some new thing to know."

(Alas! We two, we two, thou say'st!
    Yea, one wast thou with me
That once of old. But shall God lift
    To endless unity
The soul whose likeness with thy soul
    Was but its love for thee?)

"We two," she said, "will seek the groves
    Where the Lady Mary is,
With her five handmaidens, whose names
    Are five sweet symphonies,
Cecily, Gertrude, Magdalan,
    Margaret, and Rosalys.

"Circlewise sit they, with bound locks
    And foreheads garlanded:
Into the fine cloth, white like flame,
    Weaving the golden thread,
To fashion the birth-robes for them
    Who are just born, being dead.

"He shall fear, haply, and be dumb;
    Then will I lay my cheek
To his, and tell about our love,
    Not once abashed or weak:

And the dear Mother will approve
   My pride, and let me speak.

"Herself shall bring us, hand in hand,
   To Him round whom all souls
Kneel, the clear-ranged unnumbered heads
   Bowed with their aureoles:
And angels meeting us shall sing
   To their citherns and citoles.

"There will I ask of Christ the Lord
   Thus much for him and me:—
Only to live as once on earth
   With Love—only to be,
As then awhile, forever now
   Together, I and he."

She gazed and listened, and then said,
   Less sad of speech than mild—
"All this is when he comes." She ceased,
   The light thrilled towards her, filled
With angels in strong level flight,
   Her eyes prayed, and she smiled.

(I saw her smile.) But soon their path
   Was vague in distant spheres:
And then she cast her arms along
   The golden barriers,
And laid her face between her hands
   And wept. (I heard her tears.)

—DANTE GABRIEL ROSSETTI

Jane's Marriage

"The Janeites"

Jane went to Paradise:
    That was only fair.
Good Sir Walter followed her,
    And armed her up the stair.
Henry and Tobias,
    And Miguel of Spain,
Stood with Shakespeare at the top
    To welcome Jane—

When the Three Archangels
    Offered out of hand
Anything in Heaven's gift
    That she might command.
Azrael's eyes upon her,
    Raphael's wings above,
Michael's sword against her heart,
    Jane said: "Love."

Instantly the under-
    standing Seraphim
Laid their fingers on their lips
    And went to look for him.
Stole across the Zodiac,
    Harnessed Charles's Wain,
And whispered round the Nebulae
    "Who loved Jane?"

In a private limbo
    Where none had thought to look,
Sat a Hampshire gentleman
    Reading of a book.

It was called Persuasion.
  And it told the plain
Story of the love between
  Him and Jane.

He heard the question
  Circle Heaven through—
Closed the book and answered:
  "I did—and do!"
Quietly but speedily
  (As Captain Wentworth moved)
Entered into Paradise
  The man Jane loved!

—RUDYARD KIPLING

Meet Thee, Somewhere

  O ghost,
  That has gone
  Away, far away
  —To another coast,
  And another day:

  I pray
  I may
  Meet with thee there
  —In another clay,
  In another air:

  'Tis all,
  O ghost,
  I know of prayer

—To meet thee, somewhere,
Anywhere.

—JAMES STEPHENS

if there are any heavens

if there are any heavens my mother will (all by
herself) have
one. It will not be a pansy heaven or
a fragile heaven of lilies-of-the-valley but
it will be a heaven of blackred roses

my father will be (deep like a rose
tall like a rose)

standing near my

swaying over her
    (silent)
with eyes which are really petals and see
nothing with the face of a poet really which
is a flower and not a face with
hands
which whisper
This is my beloved my

(suddenly in sunlight
he will bow,

and the whole garden will bow)

—E E CUMMINGS

A Child's Dream of a Star

There was once a child, and he strolled about a good deal, and thought of a number of things. He had a sister, who was a child too, and his constant companion. These two used to wonder all day long. They wondered at the beauty of the flowers; they wondered at the height and blueness of the sky; they wondered at the depth of the bright water; they wondered at the goodness and the power of God who made the lovely world.

They used to say to one another, sometimes, supposing all the children upon earth were to die, would the flowers, and the water, and the sky be sorry? They believed they would be sorry. For, said they, the buds are the children of the flowers, and the little playful streams that gambol down the hillsides are the children of the water; and the smallest bright specks playing at hide-and-seek in the sky all night must surely be the children of the stars; and they would all be grieved to see their playmates, the children of men, no more.

There was one clear, shining star that used to come out in the sky before the rest, near the church spire, above the graves. It was larger and more beautiful, they thought, than all the others, and every night they watched for it, standing hand in hand at a window. Whoever saw it first, cried out, "I see the star!" And often they cried out both together, knowing so well when it would rise, and where. So they grew to be such friends with it, that, before lying down in their beds, they always looked out once again, to bid it good night; and when they were turning round to sleep, they used to say, "God bless the star!"

But while she was still very young, oh, very, very young, the sister drooped, and came to be so weak that she could no longer stand in the window at night; and then the child looked sadly out by himself, and when he saw the star, turned round and said to the patient pale face on the bed, "I see the star!" and then a smile would come upon the face, and a little weak voice used to say, "God bless my brother and the star!"

And so the time came, all too soon! when the child looked out alone, and when there was no face on the bed; and when there was a little grave among the graves, not there before; and when the star made long rays down toward him, as he saw it through his tears.

Now, these rays were so bright, and they seemed to make such a shining way from earth to Heaven, that when the child went to his solitary bed, he dreamed about the star; and dreamed that, lying where he was, he saw a train of people taken up that sparkling road by angels. And the star, opening, showed him a great world of light, where many more such angels waited to receive them.

All these angels, who were waiting, turned their beaming eyes upon the people who were carried up into the star; and some came out from the long rows in which they stood, and fell upon the people's necks, and kissed them tenderly, and went away with them down avenues of light, and were so happy in their company, that lying in his bed he wept for joy.

But there were many angels who did not go with them, and among them one he knew. The patient face that once had lain upon the bed was glorified and radiant, but his heart found out his sister among all the host.

His sister's angel lingered near the entrance of the star, and said to the leader among those who had brought the people thither:

"Is my brother come!"

And he said, "No."

She was turning hopefully away when the child stretched out his arms, and cried, "Oh sister, I am here! Take me!" and then she turned her beaming eyes upon him, and it was night; and the star was shining into the room, making long rays down toward him as he saw it through his tears.

From that hour forth, the child looked out upon the star as on the home he was to go to, when his time should come; and he thought that he did not belong to the earth alone, but to the star too, because of his sister's angel gone before.

There was a baby born to be a brother of the child; and while he was so little that he never yet had spoken word, he stretched his tiny form out on his bed, and died.

Again the child dreamed of the opened star, and of the company of angels, and the train of people, and the rows of angels with their beaming eyes all turned upon those people's faces.

Said his sister's angel to the leader:

"Is my brother come!"

And he said, "Not that one, but another."

As the child beheld his brother's angel in her arms, he cried, "Oh, sister, I am here! Take me!" And she turned and smiled upon him, and the star was shining.

He grew to be a young man, and was busy at his books when an old servant came to him and said:

"Thy mother is no more. I bring her blessing on her darling son!"

Again at night he saw the star, and all that former company. Said his sister's angel to the leader:

"Is my brother come?"

And he said, "Thy mother!"

A mighty cry of joy went forth through all the star, because the mother was reunited to her two children. And he stretched out his arms and cried, "Oh, mother, sister, and brother, I am here! Take me!" And they answered him, "Not yet," and the star was shining.

He grew to be a man, whose hair was turning gray, and he was sitting in his chair by the fireside, heavy with grief, and with his face bedewed with tears, when the star opened once again.

Said his sister's angel to the leader, "Is my brother come?"

And he said, "Nay, but his maiden daughter."

And the man who had been the child saw his daughter, newly lost to him, a celestial creature among those three, and he said, "My daughter's head is on my sister's bosom, and her arm is around my mother's neck, and at her feet there is the baby of old time, and I can bear the parting from her, God be praised!"

And the star was shining.

Thus the child came to be an old man, and his once smooth face was wrinkled, and his steps were slow and feeble, and his back was bent. And one night as he lay upon his bed, his children standing round, he cried as he had cried so long ago:

"I see the star!"

They whispered to one another, "He is dying."

And he said, "I am. My age is falling from me like a garment, and I move toward the star as a child. And oh, my Father, now I thank Thee that it has so often opened, to receive those dear ones who await me!"

And the star was shining; and it shines upon his grave.

—CHARLES DICKENS

CHAPTER 5
"APPARELED IN CELESTIAL LIGHT"

*"God's in his heaven, all's right with the world," trumpeted
poet Robert Browning. But others are there, too: angels, the
inhabitants of Heaven, fulfilling their duties as messengers.
What would Heaven—or Earth—be without them?
Equal in innocence to angels and as inseparable from
Paradise are children, decreed so by Jesus, who said: "Suffer
the little children to come unto me, and forbid them not:
for of such is the kingdom of God" (Mark 10:14).*

Arrival

Angels gather.
The rush of mad air
cyclones through.
Wing tips brush the
hair, a million
strands
stand; waving black anemones.
Hosannahs crush the
shell's ear tender, and
tremble
down clattering
to the floor.
Harps sound,
undulate their
sensuous meanings.
Hallelujah! Hallelujah!

You
beyond the door.

—MAYA ANGELOU

Winged Messenger

O, speak again, bright angel! for thou art
As glorious to this night, being o'er my head
As is a winged messenger of heaven
Unto the white-upturned wondering eyes
Of mortals that fall back to gaze on him
When he bestrides the lazy-pacing clouds.

—WILLIAM SHAKESPEARE
(from *Romeo and Juliet*)

The Angel

"Whenever a good child dies, an angel of God comes down from Heaven, takes the dead child in his arms, spreads out his great white wings, and flies with him over all the places which the child has loved during his life. Then he gathers a large handful of flowers which he carries up to the Almighty, that they may bloom more brightly in Heaven than they do on earth. And the Almighty presses the flowers to His heart, but He kisses the flower that pleases Him best, and it receives a voice and is able to join the song of the chorus of bliss."

These words were spoken by an angel of God as he carried a dead child up to Heaven.

—HANS CHRISTIAN ANDERSEN

Wonder

How like an angel came I down!
　　How bright are all things here!
When first among His works I did appear.
　　O how their glory me did crown!
The world resembled His eternity.
　　　　In which my soul did walk;
　　And everything that I did see
　　　　Did with me talk.

The skies in their magnificence,
　　　　The lively, lovely air,
Oh, how divine, how soft, how sweet, how fair!
　　The stars did entertain my sense;
And all the works of God so bright and pure,
　　　　So rich and great did seem
　　As if they ever must endure
　　　　In my esteem.

A native health and innocence
　　　　Within my bones did grow;
And while my God did all His glories show,
　　I felt a vigor in my sense
That was all spirit: I within did flow
　　　　With seas of life like wine;
　　I nothing in the world did know
　　　　But 'twas divine.

Harsh, ragged objects were concealed:
　　Oppressions, tears, and cries,
Sins, griefs, complaints, dissensions, weeping eyes
　　Were hid, and only things revealed
Which heavenly spirits and the angels prize.

The state of innocence
And bliss, not trades and poverties,
    Did fill my sense.

The streets were paved with golden stones;
    The boys and girls were mine:
Oh, how did all their lovely faces shine!
    The sons of men were holy ones;
In joy and beauty they appeared to me;
    And everything which here I found,
    While like an angel I did see,
        Adorned the ground.

Rich diamond and pearl and gold
    In every place was seen;
Rare splendors, yellow, blue, red, white, and green,
    Mine eyes did everywhere behold.
Great wonders clothed with glory did appear;
    Amazement was my bliss;
    That and my wealth was everywhere;
        No joy to this!

Cursed and devised proprieties,
    With envy, avarice,
And fraud (those fiends that spoil even Paradise)
    Flew from the splendor of mine eyes;
And so did hedges, ditches, limits, bounds:
    I dreamed not aught of those,
    But in surveying all men's grounds
        I found repose.

For property itself was mine,
    And hedges, ornaments:
Walls, houses, coffers, and their rich contents

To make me rich combine.
Clothes, ribbons, jewels, laces I esteemed
    My wealth by others worn;
  For me they all to wear them seemed
      When I was born.

———THOMAS TRAHERNE

Mrs. March broke the silence that followed Jo's words, by saying in her cheery voice, "Do you remember how you used to play Pilgrim's Progress when you were little things? Nothing delighted you more than to have me tie my piece-bags on your backs for burdens, give you hats and sticks and rolls of paper, and let you travel through the house from the cellar, which was the City of Destruction, up, up, to the house-top, where you had all the lovely things you could collect to make a Celestial City."

"What fun it was, especially going by the lions, fighting Apolylon, and passing through the Valley where the hobgoblins were!" said Jo.

"I liked the place where the bundles fell off and tumbled down stairs," said Meg.

"My favorite part was when we came out on the flat roof where our flowers and arbors and pretty things were, and all stood and sung for joy up there in the sunshine," said Beth, smiling, as if that pleasant moment had come back to her.

"I don't remember much about it, except that I was afraid of the cellar and the dark entry, and always liked the cake and milk we had up at the top. If I wasn't too old for such things, I'd rather like to play it over again," said Amy, who began to talk of renouncing childish things at the mature age of twelve.

"We never are too old for this, my dear, because it is a play we are playing all the time in one way or another. Our burdens are here, our road is before us, and the longing for goodness and happiness is the guide that leads us through many troubles and mistakes to the peace which is a true Celestial City. Now, my little pilgrims, suppose you begin again, not in play, but in earnest, and see how far on you can get before father comes home."

—LOUISA MAY ALCOTT
(from *Little Women*)

Little Jesus

Little Jesus was Thou shy
Once, and just as small as I?
And what did it feel like to be
Out of Heaven and just like me?
Didst Thou sometimes think of there,
And ask where all the angels were?
I should think that I would cry
For my house all made of sky;
I would look about the air,
And wonder where the angels were;
And at waking 'twould distress me—
Not an angel there to dress me!
Hadst Thou ever any toys,

Like us little girls and boys?
And didst Thou play in Heaven with all
The angels that were not too tall,
With stars for marbles? Did the things
Play "Can you see me?" through their wings?
And did Thy mother let Thee spoil
Thy robes with playing on our soil?
How nice to have them always new
In Heaven, because 'twas quite clean blue!

Didst Thou kneel at night to pray,
And didst Thou join Thy hands this way?
And did they tire sometimes, being young,
And make the prayers seem very long?
And dost Thou like it best that we
Should join our hands to pray to Thee?
I used to think before I knew,
The prayer not said unless we do.
And did Thy mother at the night
Kiss Thee and fold the clothes in right?
And didst Thou feel quite good in bed,
Kissed, and sweet, and Thy prayers said?
Thou canst not have forgotten all
That it feels like to be small:
And Thou knowest I cannot pray
To Thee in my father's way—
When Thou wast so little, say,
Couldst Thou talk in Thy Father's way?
So, a little child, come down
And hear a little child's tongue like Thy own;
Take me by the hand and walk,
And listen to my baby talk;
To Thy Father show my prayer

(He will look, Thou art so fair)
And say: O Father, I, Thy Son,
Bring the prayer of a little one;
And He will smile, the children's tongue,
Has not changed since Thou wast young.

—FRANCIS THOMPSON

Innocence

But that which most I wonder at, which most
I did esteem my bliss, which most I boast
And ever shall enjoy, is that within
  I felt no stain, nor spot of sin:

  No darkness then did overshade,
  But all within was pure and bright,
  No guilt did crush nor fear invade,
  But all my soul was full of light.

  A joyful sense and purity
   Is all I can remember.
  The very night to me was bright,
  'Twas Summer in December.

A serious meditation did employ
My soul within, which, taken up with joy,
Did seem no outward thing to note, but fly
  All objects that do feed the eye.

  While it those very objects did
  Admire, and prize, and praise, and love,
  Which in their glory most are hid,
  Which presence only doth remove.

Their constant daily presence I
    Rejoicing at, did see;
And that which takes them from the eye
Of others, offered them to me.

No inward inclination did I feel
To avarice or pride: my soul did kneel
In admiration all the day. No lust, nor strife,
    Polluted then my infant life.

    No fraud nor anger in me moved,
    No malice, jealousy or spite;
    All that I saw I truly loved.
    Contentment only and delight

    Were in my soul. O Heaven! what bliss
        Did I enjoy and feel!
    What powerful delight did this
    Inspire! for this I daily kneel.

Whether it be that nature is so pure,
And custom only vicious, or that sure
God did by miracle the guilt remove,
    And make my soul to feel his love,

    So early; Or that 'twas one day
    Where in this happiness I found,
    Whose strength and brightness so do ray,
    That still it seems me to surround:

    What e'er it is, it is a light
        So endless unto me
    That I a world of true delight
    Did then and to this day do see.

That prospect was the Gate of Heaven, that day

The ancient Light of Eden did convey
Into my soul: I was an Adam there,
> A little Adam in a sphere

> Of joys! O there my ravished sense
> Was entertained in paradise,
> And had a sight of innocence,
> Which was beyond all bound and price.

> An antepast of Heaven sure!
> > I on the Earth did reign.
> Within, without me, all was pure.
> I must become a Child again.

—THOMAS TRAHERNE

Israfel

In Heaven a spirit doth dwell
> "Whose heart-strings are a lute";
None sing so wildly well
As the angel Israfel,
And the giddy stars (so legends tell),
Ceasing their hymns, attend the spell
> Of his voice, all mute.

The ecstasies above
> With thy burning measures suit—
Thy grief, thy joy, thy hate, thy love,
> With the fervor of thy lute—
> Well may the stars be mute!

Yes, Heaven is thine; but this
> Is a world of sweet and sours;

Our flowers are merely—flowers,
And the shadow of thy perfect bliss
Is the sunshine of ours.

If I could dwell
Where Israfel
Hath dwelt, and he where I,
He might not sing so wildly well
A mortal melody,
While a bolder note than his might swell
From my lyre within the sky.

—EDGAR ALLAN POE

First and Second Childhood

Certainly Adam in Paradise had not more sweet and curious apprehensions of the world than I when I was a child. All appeared new and strange at first, inexpressibly rare and delightful and beautiful. I was a little stranger, which at my entrance into the world was saluted and surrounded with innumerable joys. My knowledge was Divine. I knew by intuition those things which since my Apostasy I collected again by the highest reason. My very ignorance was advantageous. I seemed as one brought into the Estate of Innocence.

All things were spotless and pure and glorious; yea, and infinitely mine and joyful and precious. I knew not that there were any sins or complaints or laws. I dreamed not of poverties, contentions or vices. All tears and quarrels were hidden from mine eyes. Everything was at rest, free and immortal. I knew nothing of sickness or death or rents or exaction, either for tribute or bread. In the absence of these I was entertained like an Angel with the works of God in their splendor and glory. I saw all the peace of Eden; Heaven and Earth did sing my Creator's praises, and could not make more melody to Adam than to me. All Time was Eternity and a perpetual Sabbath. Is it not strange that an infant should be heir of the whole World and see those mysteries which the books of the learned never unfold?

The corn was orient and immortal wheat, which never should be reaped, nor was ever sown. I thought it had stood from everlasting to everlasting. The dust and stones of the street were as precious as gold; the gates were at first the end of the world. The green trees when I saw them first through one of the gates transported and ravished me; their sweetness and unusual beauty made my heart to leap and almost mad with ecstasy, they were such strange and wonderful things. The Men! O what venerable and reverend creatures did the aged seem! Immortal Cherubims! And young men glittering and sparkling Angels and maids strange seraphic pieces of life and beauty! Boys and girls tumbling in the street and playing were moving jewels. I knew not that they were born or should die; but all things abided eternally as they were in their proper places. Eternity was manifest in the Light of the Day; and something infinite behind everything appeared, which talked with my expectation and moved my desire.

The city seemed to stand in Eden or to be built
in Heaven. The streets were mine, the temple was
mine, the people were mine, their clothes and gold
and silver were mine as much as their sparkling
eyes, fair skins and ruddy faces. The skies were
mine, and so were the sun and moon and stars, and
all the World was mine and I the only spectator and
enjoyer of it. I knew no churlish proprieties nor
bounds nor divisions; but all proprieties and divisions were mine, all treasures and the possessors of
them. So that with much ado I was corrupted and
made to learn the dirty devices of this world. Which
now I unlearn and become, as it were, a little child
again that I may enter into the Kingdom of God.

——THOMAS TRAHERNE

Guardian Angels of Men

And is there care in heaven? and is there love
In heavenly spirits to these creatures base,
That may compassion of their evils move?
There is: else much more wretched were the case
Of men, than beasts. But, O! th'exceeding grace
Of highest God, that loves his creatures so,
And all his works with mercy doth embrace,
That blessed angels he sends to and fro,
To serve to wicked man, to serve his wicked foe.

How oft do they their silver bowers leave,
To come to succour us, that succour want?
How oft do they with golden pinions cleave
The flitting skies, like flying pursuivant,

Against foul friends to aid us militant?
They for us fight, they watch and duly ward,
And their bright squadrons round about us plant,
And all for love, and nothing for reward:
O! why should heavenly God to men have such
regard?

—EDMUND SPENSER

Angels' Wings

"Well, Cap, what you done with your wings?"

I saw in a minute that there was some sarcasm done up in that rag somewheres, but I never let on. I only says,—

"Gone to the wash."

"Yes," he says, in a dry sort of way, "they mostly go to the wash—about this time—I've often noticed it. Fresh angels are powerful neat. When do you look for 'em back?"

"Day after tomorrow," says I.

He winked at me, and smiled.

Says I,—

"Sandy, out with it. Come—no secrets among friends. I notice you don't ever wear wings—and plenty others don't. I've been making an ass of myself—is that it?"

"That is about the size of it. But it is no harm. We all do it at first.

"It's perfectly natural. You see, on earth we jump to such foolish conclusions as to things up here. In the pictures we always saw the angels with

wings on——and that was all right; but we jumped
to the conclusion that that was their way of getting
around——and that was all wrong. The wings ain't
anything but a uniform, that's all. When they are in
the field——so to speak,—— they always wear them;
you never seen an angel going with a message anywhere without his wings, any more than you
would see a military officer presiding at a court-
martial without his uniform, or a postman deliver-
ing letters, or a policeman walking his beat, in plain
clothes. But they ain't to fly with! The wings are for
show, not for use. Old experienced angels are like
officers of the regular army——they dress plain,
when they are off duty. New angels are like the
militia——never shed the uniform——always fluttering and floundering around in their wings, butting
people down, flapping here, and there, and everywhere, always imagining they are attracting the
admiring eye——well, they just think they are the
very most important people in heaven. And when
you see one of them come sailing around with one
wing tipped up and t'other down, you make up
your mind he is saying to himself: 'I wish Mary Ann
in Arkansaw could see me now. I reckon she'd wish
she hadn't shook me.' No, they're just for show,
that's all——only just for show."

——MARK TWAIN
(from *Captain Stormfield's Visit to Heaven*)

Blest Pair of Sirens

Blest pair of Sirens, pledges of Heav'n's joy,
Sphere-born harmonious sisters, Voice, and Verse,
Wed your divine sounds, and mixed power employ
Dead things with inbreath'd sense able to pierce,
And to our high-rais'd fantasy present,
That undisturbed song of pure content,
Ay sung before the sapphire-color'd throne
To him that sits theron
With saintly shout, and solemn jubilee,
Where the bright seraphim in burning row
Their loud up-lifted angel trumpets blow,
And the cherubic host in thousand choirs
Touch their immortal harps of golden wires,
With those just spirits that wear victorious palms,
Hymns devout and holy psalms,
Singing everlastingly;
That we on earth with undiscording voice
May rightly answer that melodious noise;
As once we did, till disproportion'd sin
Jarr'd against nature's chime, and with harsh din
Broke the fair music that all creatures made
To their great Lord, whose love their motion sway'd
In perfect diapason, whilst they stood
In first obedience, and their state of good.
O may we soon again renew that song,
And keep in tune with Heav'n, till God ere long
To his celestial consort us unite,
To live with him, and sing in endless morn of light.

—JOHN MILTON

Charming Symphony

No sooner had th'Almighty ceased, but all
   The multitude of angels with a shout,
   Loud as from numbers without number, sweet
As from blest voices, uttering joy, heav'n rung
With jubilee, and loud hosannas filled
The eternal regions . . .

Then, crowned again, their golden harps they took.
   Harps ever tuned, that glittering by their side
Like quivers hung, and with preamble sweet
Of charming symphony they introduce
Their sacred song, and waken raptures high;
No voice exempt, no voice but well could join
Melodious part, such concord is in heaven.

           —JOHN MILTON
           (from *Paradise Lost*)

Jubilant Angels

And at that center, with their wings expanded,
   More than a thousand jubilant Angels saw I,
   Each differing in effulgence and in kind.
I saw there at their sports and at their songs
   A beauty smiling, which the gladness was
   Within the eyes of all the other saints;
And if I had in speaking as much wealth
   As in imagining, I should not dare
   To attempt the smallest part of its delight.

           —DANTE ALIGHIERI
           (from *Paradiso*)

The Secret of Heaven

The secret of heaven is kept from age to age. No imprudent, no sociable angel ever dropped an early syllable to answer the longings of saints, the fears of mortals.

—RALPH WALDO EMERSON

Ode on Intimations of Immortality

There was a time when meadow, grove, and stream,
The earth, and every common sight,
    To me did seem
  Appareled in celestial light,
The glory and the freshness of a dream.
It is not now as it hath been of yore;—
    Turn wheresoe'er I may,
      By night or day,
The things which I have seen I now can see no more.

    The Rainbow comes and goes,
    And lovely is the Rose,
    The Moon doth with delight
Look round her when the heavens are bare,
    Waters on a starry night
    Are beautiful and fair;
The sunshine is a glorious birth;
But yet I know, where'er I go,
    That there hath passed away a glory from
      the earth.

Now, while the birds thus sing a joyous song,
    And while the young lambs bound

  As to the tabor's sound,
 To me alone there came a thought of grief:
 A timely utterance gave that thought relief,
  And I again am strong:
 The cataracts blow their trumpets from the steep;
 No more shall grief of mine the season wrong;
 I hear the Echoes through the mountains throng,
 The Winds come to me from the fields of sleep,
  And all the earth is gay;
   Land and sea
  Give themselves up to jollity,
   And with the heart of May
  Doth every Beast keep holiday;—
   Thou Child of Joy,
Shout round me, let me hear thy shouts, thou happy
Shepherd-boy!

Ye blessed Creatures, I have heard the call
Ye to each other make; I see
The heavens laugh with you in your jubilee;
 My heart is at your festival,
 My head hath its coronal,
The fullness of your bliss, I feel—I feel it all.
 Oh evil day! if I were sullen
 While Earth herself is adorning,
  This sweet May-morning,
 And the Children are culling
  On every side,
 In a thousand valleys far and wide,
 Fresh flowers; while the sun shines warm,
And the Babe leaps up on his Mother's arm:—
 I hear, I hear, with joy I hear!
 But there's a Tree, of many, one,

A single Field which I have looked upon,
Both of them speak of something that is gone:
   The Pansy at my feet
   Doth the same tale repeat:
Whither is fled the visionary gleam?
Where is it now, the glory and the dream?

Our birth is but a sleep and a forgetting:
The Soul that rises with us, our life's Star,
   Hath had elsewhere its setting,
   And cometh from afar:
   Not in entire forgetfulness,
   And not in utter nakedness,
But trailing clouds of glory do we come
   From God, who is our home:
Heaven lies about us in our infancy!
Shades of the prison-house begin to close
   Upon the growing Boy,
But He beholds the light, and whence it flows,
   He sees it in his joy;
The Youth, who daily farther from the east
   Must travel, still is Nature's Priest,
   And by the vision splendid
   Is on his way attended;
At length the Man perceives it die away,
And fade into the light of common day.

—WILLIAM WORDSWORTH
(from *Recollections of Early Childhood*)

CHAPTER 6
"ABANDON HOPE,
ALL WHO ENTER HERE"

Is Hell the opposite of Heaven? If one is "pure and endless light," the other is full of "endless pains and sorrows" (Herman Melville). If one is "superior bliss" (John Keats), the other is a torment of "ten thousand hells in being deprived of everlasting bliss" (Christopher Marlowe). But the infernal region may embody its own contradictions. "Hell," according to Jean-Paul Sartre, is "other people"; while T. S. Eliot decrees that "Hell is oneself."

My Life Closed

My life closed twice before its close—
It yet remains to see
If Immortality unveil
A third event to me

So huge, so hopeless to conceive
As these that twice befell.
Parting is all we know of heaven,
And all we need of hell.

—EMILY DICKINSON

Face of God

Why this is hell, nor am I out of it: Thinkst thou that I who saw the face of God and tasted the eternal joys of Heaven, am not tormented with tent-thousand hells in being deprived of everlasting bliss!

—CHRISTOPHER MARLOWE
(from *Dr. Faustus*)

❦

Murder in the Cathedral

I have had a tremour of bliss, a wink of heaven, a
    whisper,
And I would no longer be denied; all things
Proceed to a joyful consummation

. . . .

The agents of hell disappear, the human, they shrink
    and dissolve
Into dust on the wind, forgotten, unmemorable;
    only is here
The white flat face of Death, God's silent servant,
And behind the face of Death the Judgement
And behind the Judgement the Void, more horrid
    than active shapes of hell;
Emptiness, absence, separation from God;
The horror of the effortless journey, to the empty
    land
Which is no land, only emptiness, absence, the Void.

—T. S. ELIOT

❦

Said the Preacher

Last and crowning torture of all the tortures of that
awful place is the eternity of hell. Eternity! O,
dread and dire word. Eternity! What mind of man

can understand it? And remember, it is an eternity of pain. Even though the pains of hell were not so terrible as they are, yet they would become infinite, as they are destined to last for ever. But while they are everlasting they are at the same time, as you know, intolerably intense, unbearably extensive. To bear even the sting of an insect for all eternity would be a dreadful torment. What must it be, then, to bear the manifold tortures of hell for ever? For ever! For all eternity! Not for a year or for an age but for ever. Try to imagine the awful meaning of this. You have often seen the sand on the seashore. How fine are its tiny grains! And how many of those tiny little grains go to make up the small handful which a child grasps in its play. Now imagine a mountain of that sand, a million miles high, reaching from the earth to the farthest heavens, and a million miles broad, extending to remotest space, and a million miles in thickness: and imagine such an enormous mass of countless particles of sand multiplied as often as there are leaves in the forest, drops of water in the mighty ocean, feathers on birds, scales on fish, hairs on animals, atoms in the vast expanse of the air: and imagine that at the end of every million years a little bird came to that mountain and carried away in its beak a tiny grain of that sand. How many millions upon millions of centuries would pass before that bird had carried away even a square foot of that mountain, how many eons upon eons of ages before it had carried away all. Yet at the end of that immense stretch of time not even one instant of eternity could be said to have ended. At the end of all those billions and trillions of years eternity would have scarcely begun. And if that mountain rose again after it had been all carried away and if the bird came again and carried it all away again grain by grain: and if it so rose and sank as many times as there are stars in the sky, atoms in the air, drops of water in the sea, leaves on the trees, feathers upon birds, scales upon fish, hairs upon animals, at the end of all those innumerable risings and sinkings of that immeasurably vast mountain not one single instant of eternity could be said to have ended; even then, at the end of such a period, after that eon of time the mere thought of which makes our very brain reel dizzily, eternity would have scarcely begun.

——JAMES JOYCE
(from *A Portrait of the Artist as a Young Man*)

To Dives

Dives, when you and I go down to Hell
Where scribblers end and millionaires as well,
We shall be carrying on our separate backs
Two very large but very different packs;
And as you stagger under yours, my friend,
Down the dull shore where all our journeys end
And go before me (as your rank demands)
Toward the infinite flat underlands,
And that dear river of forgetfulness—
Charon, a man of exquisite address

(For as your wife's progenitors could tell,
They're very strict on etiquette in Hell),
Will, since you are a lord, observe, "My lord,
We cannot take these weighty things aboard!"
Then down they go, my wretched Dives, down—
The fifteen sorts of boots you kept for town,
The hat to meet the Devil in; the plain
But costly ties; the cases of champagne;
The solid watch, and seal, and chain, and charm;
The working model of a Burning Farm
(To give the little Belials); all the three
Biscuits for Cerberus; the guarantee
From Lambeth that the rich can never burn,
And even promising a safe return;
The admirable overcoat, designed
To cross Cocytus—very warmly lined;
Sweet Dives, you will leave them all behind
And enter Hell as tattered and as bare
As was your father when he took the air
Behind a barrow-load in Leicester Square.
Then turned to me, and noting one that brings
With careless step a mist of shadowy things;
Laughter and memories, and a few regrets,
Some honor, and a quantity of debts,
A doubt or two of sorts, a trust in God,
And (what will seem to you extremely odd)
His father's granfer's father's father's name,
Unspoilt, untitled, even spelt the same;
Charon, who twenty thousand times before
Has ferried Poets to the ulterior shore,
Will estimate the weight I bear and cry—
"Comrade!" (He has himself been known to try

His hand at Latin and Italian verse
Much in the style of Vergil—only worse)
"We let such vain imaginaries pass!"
Then tell me, Dives, which will look the ass—
You, or myself? Or Charon? Who can tell?
They order things so damnably in Hell.

—HILAIRE BELLOC

The Place of the Damned

All folks who pretend to religion and grace,
Allow there's a Hell, but dispute of the place;
But if Hell may by logical rules be defined,
The place of the Damned,—I will tell you my mind.
   Wherever the Damned do chiefly abound,
Most certainly there is Hell to be found,
Damned Poets, Damned Critics, Damned
    Block-Heads, Damned Knaves,
Damned Senators bribed, Damned prostitute Slaves;
Damned Lawyers and Judges, Damned Lords and
    Damned Squires,
Damned Spies and Informers, Damned Friends and
    Damned Liars;
Damned Villains, corrupted in every station,
Damned Time-Serving Priests all over the nation;
And into the bargain, I'll readily give you,
Damned Ignorant Prelates, and Councillors Privy.
Then let us no longer by parsons be flammed,
For we know by these marks, the place of the
    Damned;

And Hell to be sure is at Paris or Rome,
How happy for us, that it is not at home.

—JONATHAN SWIFT

❧

Simon Legree—a Negro Sermon

Legree's big house was white and green.
His cotton-fields were the best to be seen.
He had strong horses and opulent cattle,
And bloodhounds bold, with chains that would rattle.
His garret was full of curious things:
Books of magic, bags of gold,
And rabbits' feet on long twine strings.
But he went down to the Devil.

Legree, he sported a brass-buttoned coat,
A snake-skin necktie, a blood-red shirt.
Legree, he had a beard like a goat,
And a thick hairy neck, and eyes like dirt.
His puffed-out cheeks were fish-belly white,
He had great long teeth, and an appetite.
He ate raw meat, 'most every meal,
And rolled his eyes till the cat would squeal.

. . . .

But he went down to the Devil.

He wore hip boots, and would wade all day
To capture his slaves that had fled away.
But he went down to the Devil.

He beat poor Uncle Tom to death
Who prayed for Legree with his last breath.
Then Uncle Tom to Eva flew,

To the high sanctoriums bright and new;
And Simon Legree stared up beneath,
And cracked his heels, and ground his teeth:
And went down to the Devil.

He crossed the yard in the storm and gloom;
He went into his grand front room.
He said, "I liked him, and don't care."
He kicked a hound, he gave a swear;
He tightened his belt, he took a lamp,
Went down cellar to the webs and damp.
There in the middle of the mouldy floor
He heaved up a slab, he found a door—
And went down to the Devil.

His lamp blew out, but his eyes burned bright.
Simon Legree stepped down all night—
Down, down to the Devil.
Simon Legree he reached the place,
He saw one half of the human race,
He saw the Devil on a wide green throne,
Gnawing the meat from a big ham-bone,
And he said to Mister Devil:

  "I see that you have much to eat—
  A red ham-bone is surely sweet.
  I see that you have lion's feet;
  I see your frame is fat and fine,
  I see you drink your poison wine—
  Blood and burning turpentine."

And the Devil said to Simon Legree;
  "I like your style, so wicked and free.
  Come sit and share my throne with me,

And let us bark and revel."
And there they sit and gnash their teeth,
And each one wears a hop-vine wreath.
They are matching pennies and shooting craps,
They are playing poker and taking naps.
And old Legree is fat and fine:
He heats the fire, he drinks the wine—
Blood and burning turpentine—

 Down, down with the Devil;

  Down, down with the Devil;

   Down, down with the Devil.

       ——VACHEL LINDSAY

Heaven and Hell

Music and silence—how I detest them both! How thankful we should be that ever since our Father entered Hell—though longer ago than humans, reckoning in light years, could express no square inch of infernal space and no moment of infernal time has been surrendered to either of those abominable forces, but all has been occupied by Noise—Noise, the grand dynamism, the audible expression of all that is exultant, ruthless, and vir-ile—Noise which alone defends us from silly qualms, despairing scruples, and impossible desires. We will make the whole universe a noise in the end. We have already made great strides in this direction as regards the Earth. The melodies and silences of Heaven will be shouted down in the end. But I admit we are not yet loud enough, or anything like it. Research is in progress.

—C. S. LEWIS
(from *The Screwtape Letters,*
written by an experienced devil to a younger one)

Of Hell

Of Hell, before the very vestibule
Of opening Orcus, sit Remorse and Grief,
And pale Disease, and sad Old Age and Fear,
And Hunger that persuades to crime, and Want:
Forms terrible to see. Suffering and Death
Inhabit here, and Death's own brother Sleep;
And the mind's evil lusts and deadly War.
Lie at the threshold, and the iron beds
Of the Eumenides; and Discord wild
Her viper-locks with bloody fillets bound.

—VIRGIL
(from the *Aeneid,* trans. by Cranch)

No Limits

Hell hath no limits, nor is circumscribed,
In one self place, but where we are is hell,
And where hell is, there must we ever be.

—CHRISTOPHER MARLOWE
(from *Doctor Faustus*)

A Place for the Wicked

DON JUAN: . . . Hell, Señora, is a place for the
wicked. The wicked are quite comfortable in it: it
was made for them. You tell me you feel no pain. I
conclude you are one of those for whom Hell
exists.

—GEORGE BERNARD SHAW
(from *Man and Superman*)

Summoner's Prologue

This friar he boasts he knows somewhat of Hell,
And God He knows that it is little wonder;
Friars and fiends are never far asunder.
For, by gad, you have oftentimes heard tell
How such a friar was snatched down into Hell
In spirit, once, and by a vision blown;
And as an angel led him up and down
To show the pains and torments that there were,
In all the place he saw no friar there.
Of other folk he saw enough in woe;
And to the angel then he questioned so:
"Now, sir," said he, "have friars such a grace
That none of them shall come into this place?"
"Nay," said the angel, "millions here are thrown!"
And unto Sathanas he led him down.
"And now has Sathanas," said he, "a tail
Broader than of a galleon is the sail.
Hold up thy tail, thou Sathanas!" said he,
"Show forth thine arse and let the friar see
Where is the nest of friars in this place!"
And ere one might go half a furlong's space.

Just as the bees come swarming from a hive,
Out of the Devil's arse-hole there did drive
Full twenty thousand friars in a rout,
And through all Hell they swarmed and ran about,
And came again, as fast as they could run,
And in his arse they crept back, every one.

—GEOFFREY CHAUCER
(from *Canterbury Tales*)

Hell Fire

Though theologians commonly affirm that the
damned are tortured by hell fire, they do not
therefore believe that they are deceived by a false
idea of a tormenting fire which God has implanted
in them, but rather that they are tortured by real
fire, for the reason that, just as the incorporeal spirit of the living man is naturally confined in the
body, so by the divine power it is easily after death
confined in corporeal fire.

—RENÉ DESCARTES
(from *Objections and Replies, VI*)

Darkness Visible

Him (Satan) The Almighty Power
Hurld headlong flaming from th' Eternal Skie
With hideous ruine and combustion down
To bottomless perdition, there to dwell
In Adamantine Chains and penal Fire,
Who durst defie th' Omnipotent to Arms.

Nine times the Space that measures Day and Night
To Mortal men, he with his horrid crew
Lay vanquisht, rowling in the fiery Gulfe
Confounded though immortal: But his doom
Reserv'd him to more wrath; for now the thought
Both of lost happiness and lasting pain
Torments him; round he throws his baleful eyes
That witness'd huge affliction and dismay
Mixt with obdurate pride and stedfast hate:
At once as far as Angels kenn he views
The dismal Situation waste and wilde,
A Dungeon horrible, on all sides round
As one great Furnace flam'd, yet from those flames
No light, but rather darkness visible
Serv'd only to discover sights of woe,
Regions of sorrow, doleful shades, where peace
And rest can never dwell, hope never comes
That comes to all; but torture without end
Still urges, and a fiery Deluge, fed
With ever-burning Sulphur unconsum'd:
Such place Eternal Justice had prepar'd
For those rebellious, here their Prison ordain'd
In utter darkness, and their portion set
As far remov'd from God and light of Heav'n
As from the Center thrice to th' utmost Pole.
O how unlike the place from whence they fell!

—JOHN MILTON
(from *Paradise Lost*)

Tomlinson

Now Tomlinson gave up the ghost at his house in
  Berkeley Square,
And a Spirit came to his bedside and gripped him by
  the hair—
A Spirit gripped him by the hair and carried him far away,
Till he heard as the roar of a rain-fed ford the roar of
  the Milky Way:
Till he heard the roar of the Milky Way die down and
  drone and cease,
And they came to the Gate within the Wall where
  Peter holds the keys.
"Stand up, stand up now, Tomlinson, and answer loud
  and high
"The good that ye did for the sake of men or ever ye
  came to die—
"The good that ye did for the sake of men on little
  Earth so lone!"
And the naked soul of Tomlinson grew white as a
  rain-washed bone.
"O I have a friend on Earth," he said, "that was my
  priest and guide,
"And well would he answer all for me if he were at my
  side."
—"For that ye strove in neighbour-love it shall be
  written fair,
"But otherwise ye wait at Heaven's Gate and not in
  Berkeley Square:
"Though we called your friend from his bed this night,
  he could not speak for you,
"For the race is run by one and one and never by two
  and two."

Then Tomlinson looked up and down, and little gain
    was there,
For the naked stars grinned overhead, and he saw that
    his soul was bare.
The Wind that blows between the Worlds, it cut him
    like a knife,
And Tomlinson took up the tale and spoke of his good
    in life,
"O this I have read in a book," he said, "and that was
    told to me,
"And this I have thought that another man thought of a
    Prince in Muscovy."
The good souls flocked like homing doves and bade
    him clear the path,
And Peter twirled the jangling Keys in weariness and
    wrath.
"Ye have read, ye have heard, ye have thought," he said,
    and the tale is yet to run:
"By the worth of the body that once ye had, give
    answer—what ha' ye done?"

The Spirit gripped him by the hair, and sun by su
    they fell
Till they came to the belt of Naughty Stars that rim
    the mouth of Hell.
The first are red with pride and wrath, the next are
    white with pain,
But the third are black with clinkered sin that cannot
    burn again.
They may hold their path, they may leave their path,
    with never a soul to mark:
They may burn or freeze, but they must not cease in
    the Scorn of the Outer Dark.

The Wind that blows between the Worlds, it nipped
him to the bone,

And he yearned to the flare of Hell-gate there as the
light of his own hearth-stone.

The Devil he sat behind the bars, where the desperate
legions drew,

But he caught the hasting Tomlinson and would not let
him through.

"Wot ye the price of good pit-coal that I must pay,"
said he,

"That ye rank yoursel' so fit for Hell and ask no leave
of me?

"I am all o'er-sib to Adam's breed that ye should give
me scorn,

"For I strove with God for your First Father the day
that he was born.

"Sit down, sit down upon the slag, and answer loud
and high

"The harm that ye did to the Sons of Men or ever you
came to die."

And Tomlinson looked up and up, and saw against the
night

The belly of a tortured star blood-red in Hell-Mouth
light;

And Tomlinson looked down and down, and saw
beneath his feet

The frontlet of a tortured star milk-white in Hell-
Mouth heat.

"O I had a love on earth," said he, "that kissed me to
my fall;

"And if ye would call my love to me I know she would
answer all."

—"All that ye did in love forbid it shall be written fair,

"But now ye wait at Hell-Mouth Gate and not in
    Berkeley Square;

"Though we whistled your love from her bed to-night,
    I trow she would not run,

"For the sin ye do by two and two ye must pay for one
    by one!"

The Wind that blows between the Worlds, it cut him
    like a knife,

And Tomlinson took up the tale and spoke of his sins
    in life:—

"Once I ha' laughed at the power of Love and twice at
    the grip of the Grave,

"And thrice I ha' patted my God on the head that men
    might call me brave."

The Devil he blew on a brandered soul and set it aside
    to cool:—

"Do ye think I would waste my good pit-coal on the
    hide of a brain-sick fool?

"I see no worth in the hobnailed mirth or the jolthead
    jest ye did

"That I should waken my gentlemen that are sleeping
    three on a grid."

Then Tomlinson looked back and forth, and there was
    little grace,

For Hell-gate filled the houseless soul with the Fear of
    Naked Space.

"Nay, this I ha' heard," quo' Tomlinson, "and this was
    noised abroad,

"And this I ha' got from a Belgian book on the word of
    a dead French lord."

—"Ye ha' heard, ye ha' read, ye ha' got, good lack!

and the tale begins afresh—

"Have ye sinned one sin for the pride o' the eye or the
sinful lust of the flesh?"

Then Tomlinson he gripped the bars and yammered,
"Let me in—

For I mind that I borrowed my neighbour's wife to sin
the deadly sin."

The Devil he grinned behind the bars, and banked the
fires high:

"Did ye read of that sin in a book?" said he; and
Tomlinson said, "Ay!"

The Devil he blew upon his nails, and the little devils
ran,

And he said: "Go husk this whimpering thief that
comes in the guise of a man:

"Winnow him out 'twixt star and star, and sieve his
proper worth:

"There's sore decline in Adam's line if this be spawn of
Earth."

The Devil he blew an outward breath, for his heart
was free from care:—

"Ye have scarce the soul of a louse," he said, "but the
roots of sin are there,

"And for that sin should ye come in were I the lord
alone,

"But sinful pride has rule inside—ay, mightier than my
own.

"Honour and Wit, fore-damned they sit, to each his
Priest and Whore;

"Nay, scarce I dare myself go there, and you they'd
torture sore.

"Ye are neither spirit nor spirk," he said; "ye are
　neither book nor brute—

"Go, get ye back to the flesh again for the sake of
　Man's repute.

"I'm all o'er-sib to Adam's breed that I should mock
　your pain,

"But look that ye win to worthier sin ere ye come
　back again.

"Get hence, the hearse is at your door—the grim
　black stallions wait—

"They bear your clay to place to-day. Speed, lest ye
　come too late!

"Go back to Earth with a lip unsealed—go back with
　an open eye,

"And carry my word to the Sons of Men or ever ye
　come to die:

"That the sin they do by two and two they must pay
　for one by one,

"And . . . the God that you took from a printed book
　be with you Tomlinson!"

—RUDYARD KIPLING

I Ponder

I ponder "What is hell?" I maintain it is the suffering of not being able to love.

—FYODOR DOSTOEVSKY

Hell Is Other People

So that's what Hell is. I'd never have believed it . . .
Do you remember, brimstone, the stake, the gridiron? . . . What a joke! No need of a gridiron. Hell,
it's other people.

——JEAN-PAUL SARTRE
(from *No Exit*)

Hell Is Oneself

Hell is oneself. Hell is alone, and the other figures in
it merely projections. There is nothing to escape from
and nothing to escape to. One is always alone . . . the
final desolation of solitude in the phantasmal world of
imagination, shuffling memories, and desires.

——T. S. ELIOT
(from *The Cocktail Party*)

In Hell There Is No Hope

In Hell there is no hope, and consequently no duty,
no work, nothing to be gained by praying, nothing
to be lost by doing what you like. Hell, in short,
being a place where you have nothing to do but
amuse yourself, is the paradise of the worthless.

——GEORGE BERNARD SHAW

Hell

Hell is neither here nor there,
Hell is not anywhere,
Hell is hard to bear.

It is so hard to dream posterity
Or haunt a ruined century
And so much easier to be.

Only the challenge to our will,
Our pride in learning any skill,
Sustains our effort to be ill.

To talk the dictionary through
Without a chance word coming true
Is more than Darwin's apes could do.

Yet pride alone could not insist
Did we not hope, if we persist,
That one day Hell might actually exist.

In time, pretending to be blind
And universally unkind
Might really send us out of our mind.

If we were really wretched and asleep
It would be then de trop to weep,
It would be natural to lie,
There'd be no living left to die.

—W. H. AUDEN

Hell and Heaven

If ye can pass His gateways,
East, west, and south and north—
Which shut in earth and heaven—
Hasten ye! pass ye forth:

But Life and Death enclose ye;
By no way shall ye pass;
A fence of flame shall stay ye,
And a moat of molten brass:

And when the sky is rended,
Red like a new-ripped hide,
There shall be no accusing,
Admitted or denied:

No yea nor nay! no questions!
The sinner's brand is sin;
Thereby shall he be known,
And flung Hell's blazing walls within:

Flung by the forelock and the feet:
"'This Hell existed not,'
Ye said. Now broil! and when ye thirst,
Drink sulphur scalding hot."

But sweet for him who was faithful,
And feared the face of his God,
Are the gardens of joy preparing,
And the gates of the Golden Abode:

Shall the wages of righteous-doing
Be less than the promise given?

Nay! but by God, the Glorious,
The debt shall be paid in heaven!

—SIR EDWIN ARNOLD

Night in Hell

I have just swallowed a terrific mouthful of poison.
—Blessed, blessed, blessed the advice I was given!
—My guts are on fire.
The power of the poison twists my arms and legs,
cripples me, drives me to the ground.
I die of thirst, I suffocate, I cannot cry.
This is Hell, eternal torment! See how the flames rise!
I burn as I ought to. Go on, Devil!

—ARTHUR RIMBAUD

The Ribs and Terrors

The ribs and terrors in the whale,
    Arched over me a dismal gloom,
While all God's sun-lit waves rolled by,
    And lift me to a deeper doom.

I saw the opening maw of hell,
    With endless pains and sorrows there;
Which none but they that feel can tell—
    Oh, I was plunging to despair.

In black distress, I called my God,
    When I could scarce believe Him mine,

He bowed His ear to my complaints—
    No more the whale did me confine.

With speed He flew to my relief,
    As on a radiant dolphin borne;
Awful, yet bright, as lightning shone
    The face of my Deliverer God.

My song for ever shall record
    That terrible, that joyful hour;
I give the glory to my God,
    His all the mercy and the power.

—HERMAN MELVILLE

The Hands of God

It is a fearful thing to fall into the hands of the living
    God.
But it is a much more fearful thing to fall out of them.
Did Lucifer fall through knowledge?
oh then, pity him, pity him that plunge!
Save me, O God, from falling into the ungodly
    knowledge
of myself as I am without God.
Let me never know, O God
let me never know what I am or should be
when I have fallen out of your hands, the hands of the
    living God.

That awful and sickening endless sinking, sinking
through the slow, corruptive levels of disintegrative
    knowledge
when the self has fallen from the hands of God

and sinks, seething and sinking, corrupt
and sinking still, in depth after depth of disintegrative
    consciousness
sinking in the endless undoing, the awful katabolism
    into the abyss!
even of the soul, fallen from the hands of God.

Save me from that, O God!
Let me never know myself apart from the living God!

—D. H. LAWRENCE

A Cap of Lead

A cap of lead across the sky
Was tight and surly drawn,
We could not find the Mighty Face,
The figure was withdrawn.

A chill came up as from a shaft,
Our noon became a well,
A thunder storm combines the charms
Of Winter and of Hell.

—EMILY DICKINSON

Evil Is Homeless

Evil has no home,
only evil has no home,
not even the home of demoniacal hell.
Hell is the home of souls lost in darkness,
even as heaven is the home of souls lost in light.

And like Persephone, or Attis
there are souls that are at home in both homes.
Not like grey Dante, colour-blind
to the scarlet and purple flowers at the doors of hell.

But evil
evil has no dwelling-place
the grey vulture, the grey hyena, corpse-eaters
they dwell in the outskirt fringes of nowhere
where the grey twilight of evil sets in.

And men that sit in machines
among spinning wheels, in an apotheosis of wheels
sit in the grey mist of movement which moves not
and going which goes not
and doing which does not
and being which is not:
that is, they sit and are evil, in evil,
grey evil, which has no path, and shows neither light
   nor dark
and has no home, no home anywhere.

—D. H. LAWRENCE

⚜

Sounds of Suffering

Now the sounds of suffering started
to flood my hearing. I'd come
where loud cries were clashing on me
(all light was snuffed out where I was),
crashing like sea under storm,
the waves and the wind in combat.
This ceaseless nether whirlwind

takes spirits into its current,
tortures them with a brutal flight.
When they attain this violence
there they shriek and complain and cry,
blaspheming the power of God.

—DANTE ALIGHIERI

The Restoration of Hell

This happened when Jesus was revealing his teaching to men.

His teaching was so clear, so easy to follow, and so evidently saved men from evil, that it seemed impossible that it should not be accepted or that anything could prevent its spreading.

Beelzebub, the father and ruler of all the devils, was alarmed. He clearly saw that his power over men would be for ever ended unless Jesus renounced his teaching. He was alarmed but did not despair, and he incited the Scribes and Pharisees, his obedient servants, to insult and torment Jesus to the utmost of their power and to advise Christ's disciples to flee and abandon him. He hoped that condemnation to a shameful execution, revilings, abandonment by all his disciples, and finally the suffering and execution itself, would cause Christ at the last moment to renounce his teaching, and that such a renunciation would destroy all its power.

The matter was decided on the cross. When Christ exclaimed: "My God, my God, why hast thou forsaken me?" Beelzebub exulted. He seized the fetters prepared for Jesus, tried them on his own legs, and proceeded to adjust them so that when affixed to Jesus they could not be undone.

But suddenly the words were heard from the cross: "Father, forgive them, for they know not what they do." And after that Christ cried: "It is finished!" and gave up the ghost.

Beelzebub understood that all was lost. He wished to free his legs from the fetters and escape, but could not move from the spot. The fetters had become welded on him and bound his own limbs. He tried to use his wings, but could not unfold them. And Beelzebub saw how Christ appeared at the gates of Hell in a halo of light, and how the sinners, from Adam to Judas, came out, how all the devils fled, and how the very walls of Hell silently collapsed on all four sides. He could endure this no longer and with a piercing shriek fell through the rent floor to the nether regions.

❧

One hundred, two hundred, three hundred years passed.

Beelzebub did not count the time. Around him was black darkness and dead silence. He lay motionless and tried not to think of what had happened, yet he still thought, and impotently hated him who had caused his downfall.

But suddenly—he did not remember or know how many hundred years had elapsed—he heard above him sounds resembling the trampling of feet, groans, cries, and gnashing of teeth.

Beelzebub lifted his head and began to listen.

That Hell could be re-established after Christ's victory was more than he could believe; yet the trampling, the groans, the cries and gnashing of teeth, sounded clearer and clearer.

He raised his body and doubled up his shaggy legs with their overgrown hoofs (to his astonishment the fetters fell off of themselves), and freely flapping his extended wings he gave the whistle by which in former times he had summoned his servants and assistants around him.

Before he had time to draw breath an opening yawned above his head, red flames glared, and a crowd of devils, hustling one another, dropped through the opening into that nether region and settled around Beelzebub like birds of prey around carrion.

There were large devils and small devils, fat devils and thin devils, devils with long tails and devils with short tails, devils with pointed horns, devils with straight horns, and devils with crooked horns.

A shiny black one, naked except for a cape thrown over his shoulders, with a round hairless face and an enormous hanging paunch, sat on his heels before Beelzebub's very face, and rolling his eyes now up and now down, continued to smile, waving his long thin tail rhythmically from side to side.

"What does that noise mean?" said Beelzebub, pointing upwards. "What is going on up there?"

"Just what there always used to be," replied the shiny devil in the cape.

"Are there really some sinners?" asked Beelzebub.

"Many," replied the shiny one.

"But how about the teaching of him whom I do not wish to name?" asked Beelzebub.

The devil in the cape gave a grin that showed his sharp teeth, while suppressed laughter was heard among all the other devils.

"That teaching doesn't hinder us at all. Men don't believe in it," said the devil in the cape.

"But it plainly saved them from us, and he sealed it by his death!" said Beelzebub.

"I have altered all that," said the devil in the cape, rapidly tapping the floor with his tail.

"How have you altered it?"

"I have arranged it so that men do not believe in his teaching but in mine, which they call by his name."

—LEO TOLSTOY

CHAPTER 7
"EYE HATH NOT SEEN, NOR EAR HEARD"

Most of what we know about Heaven and Hell has come—"through a glass, darkly"—from the Bible. Down through the centuries the following passages from the Old and New Testaments have shaped human thinking—and inspired great writers—on the ultimate topics of Heaven and Hell. Consider these immortal images (quoted from the King James Version): "In my Father's house are many mansions," "a better country," "eye hath not seen, nor ear heard," "wailing and gnashing of teeth."

HEAVEN IN HOLY SCRIPTURE

Old Testament

In the beginning God created the heaven and the earth.

—GENESIS 1:1

And God called the firmament Heaven.

—GENESIS 1:8

Look down from thy holy habitation, from heaven, and bless thy people Israel, and the land which thou hast given us, as thou swarest unto our fathers, a land that floweth with milk and honey.

—DEUTERONOMY 26:15

And hearken thou to the supplication of thy servant, and of thy people Israel, when they shall pray toward this place: and hear thou in heaven thy dwelling place: and when thou hearest, forgive.

—1 KINGS 8:30

There the wicked cease from troubling; and there the weary be at rest.

—JOB 3:17

Is not God in the height of heaven? and behold the height of the stars, how high they are!

—JOB 22:12

The heavens declare the glory of God; and the firmament sheweth his handywork.

—PSALM 19:1

Whom have I in heaven but thee? and there is none upon earth that I desire beside thee.

—PSALM 73:25

Glorious things are spoken of thee, O city of God.

—PSALM 87:3

And the ransomed of the LORD shall return, and come to Zion with songs and everlasting joy upon their heads: they shall obtain joy and gladness, and sorrow and sighing shall flee away.

—ISAIAH 35:10

They shall not hunger nor thirst; neither shall the heat nor sun smite them: for he that hath mercy on them shall lead them, even by the springs of water shall he guide them.

—ISAIAH 49:10

For thus saith the high and lofty One that inhabiteth eternity, whose name is Holy; I dwell in the high and holy place, with him also that is of a contrite and humble spirit, to revive the spirit of the humble, and to revive the heart of the contrite ones.

—ISAIAH 57:15

Thy sun shall no more go down; neither shall thy moon withdraw itself: for the LORD shall be thine everlasting light, and the days of thy mourning shall be ended. Thy people also shall be all righteous: they shall inherit the land for ever, the branch of my planting, the work of my hands, that I may be glorified.

—ISAIAH 60:20–21

For, behold, I create new heavens and a new earth: and the former shall not be remembered, nor come into mind.

—ISAIAH 65:17

And I will rejoice in Jerusalem, and joy in my people: and the voice of weeping shall be no more heard in her, nor the voice of crying.

—ISAIAH 65:19

Thus saith the LORD, The heaven is my throne, and the earth is my footstool: where is the house that ye build unto me? and where is the place of my rest?

—ISAIAH 66:1

New Testament

And Jesus, when he was baptized, went up straightway out of the water: and, lo, the heavens were opened unto him, and he saw the Spirit of God descending like a dove, and lighting upon him.

—MATTHEW 3:16

Blessed are the poor in spirit: for theirs is the kingdom of heaven.

—MATTHEW 5:3

After this manner therefore pray ye: Our Father which art in heaven, Hallowed be thy name.

—MATTHEW 6:9

And I say unto you, That many shall come from the east and west, and shall sit down with Abraham, and Isaac, and Jacob, in the kingdom of heaven.

—MATTHEW 8:11

And from the days of John the Baptist until now the kingdom of heaven suffereth violence, and the violent take it by force.

—MATTHEW 11:12

Another parable put he forth unto them, saying, The kingdom of heaven is likened unto a man which sowed good seed in his field: But while men slept, his enemy came and sowed tares among the wheat, and went his way. But when the blade was sprung up, and brought forth fruit, then appeared the tares also. So the servants of the householder came and said unto him, Sir, didst not thou sow good seed in thy field? from whence then hath it tares? He said unto them, An enemy hath done this. The servants said unto him, Wilt thou then that we go and gather them up?

But he said, Nay; lest while ye gather up the tares, ye root up also the wheat with them. Let both grow together until the harvest: and in the time of harvest I will say to the reapers, Gather ye together first the tares, and bind them in bundles to burn them: but gather the wheat into my barn.

—MATTHEW 13:24–30

But Jesus said, Suffer little children, and forbid them not, to come unto me: for of such is the king-dom of heaven. And he laid his hands on them, and departed thence.

—MATTHEW 19:14–15

And Jesus said unto them, Verily I say unto you, That ye which have followed me, in the regenera-tion when the Son of man shall sit in the throne of his glory, ye also shall sit upon twelve thrones, judging the twelve tribes of Israel. And every one that hath forsaken houses, or brethren, or sisters, or father, or mother, or wife, or children, or lands, for my name's sake, shall receive an hundredfold, and shall inherit everlasting life.

—MATTHEW 19:28–29

Then shall the King say unto them on his right hand, Come, ye blessed of my Father, inherit the kingdom prepared for you from the foundation of the world.

—MATTHEW 25:34

And these shall go away into everlasting punishment: but the righteous into life eternal.

—MATTHEW 25:46

And, behold, a certain lawyer stood up, and tempted him, saying, Master, what shall I do to inherit eternal life? He said unto him, What is written in the law? how readest thou? And he answering said, Thou shalt love the Lord thy God with all thy heart, and with all thy soul, and with all thy strength, and with all thy mind; and thy neighbour as thyself. And he said unto him, Thou hast answered right: this do, and thou shalt live.

—LUKE 10:25–28

In my Father's house are many mansions: if it were not so, I would have told you. I go to prepare a place for you. And if I go and prepare a place for you, I will come again, and receive you unto myself; that where I am, there ye may be also.

—JOHN 14:2–3

And he said unto them, It is not for you to know the times or the seasons, which the Father hath put

in his own power. But ye shall receive power, after
that the Holy Ghost is come upon you: and ye shall
be witnesses unto me both in Jerusalem, and in all
Judaea, and in Samaria, and unto the uttermost
part of the earth. And when he had spoken these
things, while they beheld, he was taken up; and a
cloud received him out of their sight. And while
they looked stedfastly toward heaven as he went
up, behold, two men stood by them in white
apparel; Which also said, Ye men of Galilee, why
stand ye gazing up into heaven? this same Jesus,
which is taken up from you into heaven, shall so
come in like manner as ye have seen him go into
heaven.

—ACTS 1:7–11

And said, Behold, I see the heavens opened, and
the Son of man standing on the right hand of God.

—ACTS 7:56

And saw heaven opened, and a certain vessel
descending unto him, as it had been a great sheet
knit at the four corners, and let down to the earth.

—ACTS 10:11

But as it is written, Eye hath not seen, nor ear
heard, neither have entered into the heart of man,
the things which God hath prepared for them that
love him.

—1 CORINTHIANS 2:9

Know ye not that they which run in a race run all,
but one receiveth the prize? So run, that ye may

obtain. And every man that striveth for the mastery is temperate in all things. Now they do it to obtain a corruptible crown; but we an incorruptible.

—1 CORINTHIANS 9:24–25

For we know in part, and we prophesy in part. But when that which is perfect is come, then that which is in part shall be done away. When I was a child, I spake as a child, I understood as a child, I thought as a child: but when I became a man, I put away childish things. For now we see through a glass, darkly; but then face to face: now I know in part; but then shall I know even as also I am known.

—1 CORINTHIANS 13:9–12

For we know that if our earthly house of this tabernacle were dissolved, we have a building of God, an house not made with hands, eternal in the heavens.

—2 CORINTHIANS 5:1

It is not expedient for me doubtless to glory. I will come to visions and revelations of the Lord. I knew a man in Christ above fourteen years ago, (whether in the body, I cannot tell; or whether out of the body, I cannot tell: God knoweth;) such an one caught up to the third heaven. And I knew such a man, (whether in the body, or out of the body, I cannot tell: God knoweth;) How that he was caught up into paradise, and heard unspeakable words, which it is not lawful for a man to utter.

—2 CORINTHIANS 12:1–4

For our conversation is in heaven; from whence also we look for the Saviour, the Lord Jesus Christ: Who shall change our vile body, that it may be fashioned like unto his glorious body, according to the working whereby he is able even to subdue all things unto himself.

—PHILIPPIANS 3:20–21

If ye then be risen with Christ, seek those things which are above, where Christ sitteth on the right hand of God. Set your affection on things above, not on things on the earth.

—COLOSSIANS 3:1–2

There remaineth therefore a rest to the people of God.

—HEBREWS 4:9

For they that say such things declare plainly that they seek a country. And truly, if they had been mindful of that country from whence they came out, they might have had opportunity to have returned. But now they desire a better country, that is, an heavenly: wherefore God is not ashamed to be called their God: for he hath prepared for them a city.

—HEBREWS 11:14–16

For here have we no continuing city, but we seek one to come.

—HEBREWS 13:14

Blessed be the God and Father of our Lord Jesus Christ, which according to his abundant mercy hath begotten us again unto a lively hope by the resurrection of Jesus Christ from the dead, to an inheritance incorruptible, and undefiled, and that fadeth not away, reserved in heaven for you.

——I PETER 1:3–4

Beloved, now are we the sons of God, and it doth not yet appear what we shall be: but we know that, when he shall appear, we shall be like him; for we shall see him as he is.

——I JOHN 3:2

To him that overcometh will I grant to sit with me in my throne, even as I also overcame, and am set down with my Father in his throne.

——REVELATION 3:21

After this I beheld, and, lo, a great multitude, which no man could number, of all nations, and kindreds, and people, and tongues, stood before the throne, and before the Lamb, clothed with white robes, and palms in their hands.

——REVELATION 7:9

Therefore are they before the throne of God, and serve him day and night in his temple: and he that sitteth on the throne shall dwell among them. They shall hunger no more, neither thirst any more; neither shall the sun light on them, nor any heat. For the Lamb which is in the midst of the throne shall feed them, and shall lead them unto living fountains of waters: and God shall wipe away all tears from their eyes.

—REVELATION 7:15–17

And I beheld, and heard an angel flying through the midst of heaven, saying with a loud voice, Woe, woe, woe, to the inhabiters of the earth by reason of the other voices of the trumpet of the three angels, which are yet to sound!

—REVELATION 8:13

And I saw another angel fly in the midst of heaven, having the everlasting gospel to preach unto them that dwell on the earth, and to every nation, and kindred, and tongue, and people.

—REVELATION 14:6

And I saw a new heaven and a new earth: for the first heaven and the first earth were passed away; and there was no more sea. And I John saw the holy city, new Jerusalem, coming down from God out of heaven, prepared as a bride adorned for her husband. And I heard a great voice out of heaven saying, Behold, the tabernacle of God is with men, and he will dwell with them, and they shall be his people, and God himself shall be with them, and be their God. And God shall wipe away all tears from their eyes; and there shall be no more death, neither sorrow, nor crying, neither shall there be any more pain: for the former things are passed away. And he that sat upon the throne said, Behold, I make all things new. And he said unto me, Write: for these words are true and faithful. And he said unto me, It is done. I am Alpha and Omega, the beginning and the end. I will give unto him that is athirst of the fountain of the water of life freely. He that overcometh shall inherit all things; and I will be his God, and he shall be my son. But the fearful, and unbelieving, and the abominable, and murderers, and whoremongers, and sorcerers, and idolaters, and all liars, shall have their part in the lake which burneth with fire and brimstone: which is the second death.

—REVELATION 21:1–8

And he carried me away in the spirit to a great and high mountain, and shewed me that great city, the holy Jerusalem, descending out of heaven from God, having the glory of God: and her light was like unto a stone most precious, even like a jasper stone, clear as crystal; and had a wall great and high, and had twelve gates, and at the gates twelve angels, and names written thereon, which are the names of the twelve tribes of the children of Israel: on the east three gates; on the north three gates; on the south three gates; and on the west three gates. And the wall of the city had twelve foundations, and in them the names of the twelve apostles of the Lamb. And he that talked with me had a golden reed to measure the city, and the gates thereof, and the wall thereof. And the city lieth foursquare, and the length is as large as the breadth: and he measured the city with the reed, twelve thousand furlongs. The length and the breadth and the height of it are equal. And he measured the wall thereof, an hundred and forty and four cubits, according to the

measure of a man, that is, of the angel. And the
building of the wall of it was of jasper: and the city
was pure gold, like unto clear glass. And the foundations of the wall of the city were garnished with
all manner of precious stones. The first foundation
was jasper; the second, sapphire; the third, a chal-
cedony; the fourth, an emerald; the fifth, sar-
donyx; the sixth, sardius; the seventh, chrysolyte;
the eighth, beryl; the ninth, a topaz; the tenth, a
chrysoprasus; the eleventh, a jacinth; the twelfth,
an amethyst. And the twelve gates were twelve
pearls; every several gate was of one pearl: and the
street of the city was pure gold, as it were transparent glass. And I saw no temple therein: for the
Lord God Almighty and the Lamb are the temple
of it. And the city had no need of the sun, neither
of the moon, to shine in it: for the glory of God did
lighten it, and the Lamb is the light thereof. And
the nations of them which are saved shall walk in
the light of it: and the kings of the earth do bring
their glory and honour into it. And the gates of it
shall not be shut at all by day: for there shall be no
night there. And they shall bring the glory and honour of the nations into it. And there shall in no wise
enter into it any thing that defileth, neither whatsoever worketh abomination, or maketh a lie: but
they which are written in the Lamb's book of life.

—REVELATION 21:10–27

And there shall be no more curse: but the throne
of God and of the Lamb shall be in it; and his servants shall serve him: And they shall see his face;

and his name shall be in their foreheads. And there shall be no night there; and they need no candle, neither light of the sun; for the Lord God giveth them light: and they shall reign for ever and ever.

—REVELATION 22:3–5

HELL IN HOLY SCRIPTURE

Old Testament

For a fire is kindled in mine anger, and shall burn unto the lowest hell, and shall consume the earth with her increase, and set on fire the foundations of the mountains.

—DEUTERONOMY 32:22

The sorrows of hell compassed me about; the snares of death prevented me.

—2 SAMUEL 22:6

As the cloud is consumed and vanisheth away: so he that goeth down to the grave shall come up no more.

—JOB 7:9

They shall go down to the bars of the pit, when our rest together is in the dust.

—JOB 17:16

Hell is naked before him, and destruction hath no covering.

—JOB 26:6

For in death there is no remembrance of thee: in the grave who shall give thee thanks?

—PSALM 6:5

The wicked shall be turned into hell, and all the nations that forget God.

—PSALM 9:17

Let death seize upon them, and let them go down quick into hell: for wickedness is in their dwellings, and among them.

—PSALM 55:15

Thou hast laid me in the lowest pit, in darkness, in the deeps.

—PSALM 88:6

Her house is the way to hell, going down to the chambers of death.

—PROVERBS 7:27

Hell and destruction are never full; so the eyes of man are never satisfied.

—PROVERBS 27:20

Whatsoever thy hand findeth to do, do it with thy might; for there is no work, nor device, nor knowledge, nor wisdom, in the grave, whither thou goest.

—ECCLESIASTES 9:10

Therefore hell hath enlarged herself, and opened her mouth without measure: and their glory, and their multitude, and their pomp, and he that rejoiceth, shall descend into it.

—ISAIAH 5:14

Hell from beneath is moved for thee to meet thee at thy coming: it stirreth up the dead for thee, even all the chief ones of the earth; it hath raised up from their thrones all the kings of the nations.

—ISAIAH 14:9

Because ye have said, We have made a covenant with death, and with hell are we at agreement; when the overflowing scourge shall pass through, it shall not come unto us: for we have made lies our refuge, and under falsehood have we hid ourselves: Therefore thus saith the LORD God, Behold, I lay in Zion for a foundation a stone, a tried stone, a precious corner stone, a sure foundation; he that believeth shall not make haste. Judgment also will I lay to the line, and righteousness to the plummet: and the hail shall sweep away the refuge of lies, and the waters shall overflow the hiding place. And your covenant with death shall be disannulled, and your agreement with hell shall not stand; when the overflowing scourge shall pass through, then ye shall be trodden down by it.

—ISAIAH 28:15–18

I made the nations to shake at the sound of his fall, when I cast him down to hell with them that descend into the pit: and all the trees of Eden, the choice and best of Lebanon, all that drink water, shall be comforted in the nether parts of the earth. They also went down into hell with him unto them that be slain with the sword; and they that were his arm, that dwelt under his shadow in the midst of the heathen.

—EZEKIEL 31:16–17

The strong among the mighty shall speak to him out of the midst of hell with them that help him: they are gone down, they lie uncircumcised, slain by the sword.

—EZEKIEL 32:21

Though they dig into hell, thence shall mine hand take them; though they climb up to heaven, thence will I bring them down.

—AMOS 9:2

New Testament

And fear not them which kill the body, but are not able to kill the soul: but rather fear him which is able to destroy both soul and body in hell.

—MATTHEW 10:28

And thou, Capernaum, which art exalted unto heaven, shalt be brought down to hell: for if the mighty works, which have been done in thee, had been done in Sodom, it would have remained until this day.

—MATTHEW 11:23

And I say also unto thee, That thou art Peter, and upon this rock I will build my church; and the gates of hell shall not prevail against it.

—MATTHEW 16:18

Woe unto you, scribes and Pharisees, hypocrites! for ye compass sea and land to make one proselyte, and when he is made, ye make him twofold more the child of hell than yourselves.

—MATTHEW 23:15

Then shall he say also unto them on the left hand, Depart from me, ye cursed, into everlasting fire, prepared for the devil and his angels.

—MATTHEW 25:41

And in hell he lift up his eyes, being in torments, and seeth Abraham afar off, and Lazarus in his bosom.

—LUKE 16:23

And the tongue is a fire, a world of iniquity: so is the tongue among our members, that it defileth the whole body, and setteth on fire the course of nature; and it is set on fire of hell.

—JAMES 3:6

For if God spared not the angels that sinned, but cast them down to hell, and delivered them into chains of darkness, to be reserved unto judgment.

—2 PETER 2:4

And whosoever was not found written in the book
of life was cast into the lake of fire.

—REVELATION 20:15

CHAPTER 8
"A NEW HEAVEN AND
A NEW EARTH"

*The Bible closes not with a whimper but with a bang. The
Revelation of St. John the Divine trumpets the attributes
of the Apocalypse: tumult, lightning, violence, destruction.
But the controlling force of our powerful and loving God
reasserts itself, and a "new heaven and a new earth" are
born. This is the millennial promise.*

To God

Do with me, God! as Thou didst deal with John,
(Who writ that heavenly Revelation)
Let me (like him) first cracks of thunder hear;
Then let the harp's enchantments strike mine ear;
Here give me thorns; there, in thy Kingdom, set
Upon my head the golden coronet;
There give me day; but here my dreadful night:
My sackcloth here; but there my stole of white.

——ROBERT HERRICK

And one of the elders answered, saying unto me,
What are these which are arrayed in white robes?
and whence came they? And I said unto him, Sir,
thou knowest. And he said to me, These are they
which came out of great tribulation, and have
washed their robes, and made them white in the

blood of the Lamb. Therefore are they before the throne of God, and serve him day and night in his temple: and he that sitteth on the throne shall dwell among them. They shall hunger no more, neither thirst any more; neither shall the sun light on them, nor any heat. For the Lamb which is in the midst of the throne shall feed them, and shall lead them unto living fountains of waters: and God shall wipe away all tears from their eyes.

—REVELATION 7:13–17

General William Booth Enters into Heaven

(General Booth [1829–1912] was founder and commander in chief of the Salvation Army. To be sung to the tune of "The Blood of the Lamb" with indicated instruments.)

(Bass drums beaten loudly.)

Booth led boldly with his big bass drum—
(Are you washed in the blood of the Lamb?)
The Saints smiled gravely, and they said: "He's come."
(Are you washed in the blood of the Lamb?)
Walking lepers followed, rank on rank,
Lurching bravos from the ditches dank,
Drabs from the alleyways and drug fiends pale—
Minds still passion-ridden, soul-powers frail:—
Vermin-eaten saints with moldy breath
Unwashed legions with the ways of Death—
(Are you washed in the blood of the Lamb?)

(Banjos.)

> Every slum had sent its half-a-score
> The round world over. (Booth had groaned for more.)
> Every banner that the wide world flies
> Bloomed with glory and transcendent dyes.
> Big-voiced lassies made their banjos bang,
> Tranced, fanatical, they shrieked and sang:—
> *("Are you washed in the blood of the Lamb?")*

> Hallelujah! It was queer to see
> Bull-necked convicts with that land make free!
> Loons with trumpets blowed a blare, blare, blare
> On, on, upward through the golden air!
> *("Are you washed in the blood of the Lamb?")*

(Bass drum slower and softer.)

> Booth died blind and still by faith he trod,
> Eyes still dazzled by the ways of God.
> Booth led boldly, and he looked the chief
> Eagle countenance in sharp relief,
> Beard a-flying, air of high command
> Unabated in that holy land.

(Sweet flute music.)

> Jesus came from out the court-house door
> Stretched his hands above the passing poor
> Booth saw not, but led his queer ones there
> Round and round the mighty court-house square.
> Then, in an instant all that blear review
> Marched on spotless, clad in raiment new.
> The lame were straightened, withered limbs uncurled
> And blind eyes opened on a new, sweet world.

(Bass drum louder.)

> Drabs and vixens in a flash made whole!
> Gone was the weaselhead, the snout, the jowl!
> Sages and sibyls now, and athletes clean,
> Rulers of empires, and of forests green!

(Grand chorus of all instruments.
Tambourines to the foreground.)

> The hosts were sandalled, and their wings were fire!
> *("Are you washed in the blood of the Lamb?")*
> But their noise played havoc with the angel-choir.
> *("Are you washed in the blood of the Lamb?")*
> Oh, shout Salvation! It was good to see
> Kings and Princes by the Lamb set free.
> The banjos rattled and the tambourines
> Jing-jing-jingled in the hands of Queens.

(Reverently sung, no instruments.)

> And when Booth halted by the curb for prayer
> He saw his Master through the flag-filled air.
> Christ came gently with a robe and crown
> For Booth the soldier, while the throng knelt down.
> He saw King Jesus. They were face to face,
> And he knelt a-weeping in the holy place.
> *("Are you washed in the blood of the Lamb?")*

—VACHEL LINDSAY

And when he had opened the seventh seal, there
was silence in heaven about the space of half an

hour. And I saw the seven angels which stood before God; and to them were given seven trumpets. And another angel came and stood at the altar, having a golden censer; and there was given unto him much incense, that he should offer it with the prayers of all saints upon the golden altar which was before the throne. And the smoke of the incense which came with the prayers of the saints, ascended up before God out of the angel's hand. And the angel took the censer, and filled it with fire of the altar, and cast it into the earth: and there were voices, and thunderings, and lightnings, and an earthquake. And the seven angels which had the seven trumpets prepared themselves to sound.

—REVELATION 8:1–6

Holy Sonnet VII

At the round Earth's imagined corners, blow
Your trumpets, Angels, and arise, arise
From death, you numberless infinities
Of souls, and to your scattered bodies go,
All whom the flood did, and fire shall o'erthrow,
All whom war, dearth, age, agues, tyrannies,
Despair, law, chance, hath slain, and you whose eyes,
Shall behold God, and never taste death's woe.
But let them sleep, Lord, and me mourn a space,
For, if above all these, my sins abound,
'Tis late to ask abundance of thy grace,
When we are there; here on this lowly ground,

Teach me how to repent; for that's as good
As if thou hadst sealed my pardon, with thy blood.

—JOHN DONNE

A Wife

A Wife—at Daybreak I shall be—
Sunrise—Hast thou a Flag for me?
At Midnight, I am but a Maid,
How short it takes to make a Bride—
Then—Midnight, I have passed from thee
Unto the East, and Victory—

Midnight—Good Night! I hear them call,
The Angels bustle in the Hall—
Softly my Future climbs the Stair,
I fumble at my Childhood's prayer
So soon to be a Child no more—
Eternity, I'm coming—Sir,
Savior—I've seen the face—before!

—EMILY DICKINSON

And there appeared a great wonder in heaven; a
woman clothed with the sun, and the moon under
her feet, and upon her head a crown of twelve
stars: And she being with child cried, travailing in
birth, and pained to be delivered. And there
appeared another wonder in heaven; and behold a
great red dragon, having seven heads and ten
horns, and seven crowns upon his heads. And his

tail drew the third part of the stars of heaven, and
did cast them to the earth: and the dragon stood
before the woman which was ready to be delivered, for to devour her child as soon as it was born.
And she brought forth a man child, who was to
rule all nations with a rod of iron: and her child was
caught up unto God, and to his throne. And the
woman fled into the wilderness, where she hath a
place prepared of God, that they should feed her
there a thousand two hundred and threescore days.

—REVELATION 12:1–6

The Mental Traveller

I travelled through a Land of Men,
A Land of Men and Women too,
And heard and saw such dreadful things
As cold Earth wanderers never knew.

For there the Babe is born in joy
That was begotten in dire woe;
Just as we Reap in joy the fruit
Which we in bitter tears did sow.

And if the Babe is born a Boy
He's given to a Woman Old,
Who nails him down upon a rock,
Catches his shrieks in cups of gold.

She binds iron thorns around his head,
She pierces both his hands and feet,
She cuts his heart out at his side
To make it feel both cold and heat.

Her fingers number every Nerve,
Just as a Miser counts his gold;
She lives upon his shrieks and cries,
And she grows young as he grows old.

Till he becomes a bleeding youth,
And she becomes a Virgin bright;
Then he rends up his Manacles
And binds her down for his delight.

He plants himself in all her Nerves,
Just as a Husbandman his mould;
And she becomes his dwelling place
And Garden fruitful seventy fold.

An aged Shadow, soon he fades,
Wand'ring round an Earthly Cot,
Full filled all with gems and gold
Which he by industry had got.

And these are the gems of the Human Soul,
The rubies and pearls of a lovesick eye,
The countless gold of the aching heart,
The martyr's groan and the lover's sigh.

They are his meat, they are his drink;
He feeds the Beggar and the Poor
And the wayfaring Traveller:
For ever open is his door.

His grief is their eternal joy;
They make the roofs and walls to ring;
Till from the fire on the hearth
A little Female Babe does spring.

And she is all of solid fire

And gems and gold, that none his hand
Dares stretch to touch her Baby form
Or wrap her in his swaddling-band.

But she comes to the Man she loves,
If young or old, or rich or poor;
They soon drive out the aged Host,
A Beggar at another's door.

He wanders weeping far away,
Until some other take him in;
Oft blind and age-bent, sore distrest,
Until he can a Maiden win.

And to allay his freezing Age
The Poor Man takes her in his arms;
The Cottage fades before his sight,
The Garden and its lovely Charms.

The Guests are scattered through the land,
For the Eye altering alters all;
The Senses roll themselves in fear,
And the flat Earth becomes a Ball;

The stars, sun, moon, all shrink away,
A desart vast without a bound,
And nothing left to eat or drink,
And a dark desart all around.

The honey of her Infant lips,
The bread and wine of her sweet smile,
The wild game of her roving Eye,
Does him to Infancy beguile;

For as he eats and drinks he grows
Younger and younger every day;

And on the desart wild they both
Wander in terror and dismay.

Like the wild Stag she flees away,
Her fear plants many a thicket wild;
While he pursues her night and day,
By various arts of Love beguiled,

By various arts of Love and Hate,
Till the wide desart planted o'er
With Labyrinths of wayward Love,
Where roam the Lion, Wolf and Boar,

Till he becomes a wayward Babe,
And she a weeping Woman Old.
Then many a Lover wanders here;
The Sun and Stars are nearer rolled.

The trees bring forth sweet Extacy
To all who in the desert roam;
Till many a City there is Built,
And many a pleasant Shepherd's home.

But when they find the frowning Babe,
Terror strikes through the region wide:
They cry "The Babe! the Babe is Born!"
And flee away on Every side.

For who dare touch the frowning form,
His arm is withered to its root;
Lions, Boars, Wolves, all howling flee,
And every Tree does shed its fruit.
And none can touch that frowning form,
Except it be a Woman Old;

She nails him down upon the Rock,
And all is done as I have told.

——WILLIAM BLAKE

And I stood upon the sand of the sea, and saw a
beast rise up out of the sea, having seven heads and
ten horns, and upon his horns ten crowns, and
upon his heads the name of blasphemy. And the
beast which I saw was like unto a leopard, and his
feet were as the feet of a bear, and his mouth as the
mouth of a lion: and the dragon gave him his
power, and his seat, and great authority. And I saw
one of his heads as it were wounded to death; and
his deadly wound was healed: and all the world
wondered after the beast.

——REVELATION 13:1–3

Sonnet XII

I saw an ugly beast come from the sea,
That seven heads, ten crowns, ten horns did bear,
Having thereon the vile blaspheming name.
The cruel leopard she resembled much:
Feet of a bear, a lion's throat she had.
The mighty dragon gave to her his power.
One of her heads yet there I did espy,
Still freshly bleeding of a grievous wound.
One cried aloud. What one is like (quoth he)

This honored dragon, or may him withstand?
And then came from the sea a savage beast,
With dragon's speech, and showed his force by fire,
With wondrous signs to make all wights adore
The beast, in setting of her image up.

—EDMUND SPENSER

And there came one of the seven angels which had the seven vials, and talked with me, saying unto me, Come hither; I will shew unto thee the judgment of the great whore that sitteth upon many waters: with whom the kings of the earth have committed fornication, and the inhabitants of the earth have been made drunk with the wine of her fornication. So he carried me away in the spirit into the wilderness: and I saw a woman sit upon a scarlet coloured beast, full of names of blasphemy, having seven heads and ten horns. And the woman was arrayed in purple and scarlet colour, and decked with gold and precious stones and pearls, having a golden cup in her hand full of abominations and filthiness of her fornication: And upon her forehead was a name written, MYSTERY, BABYLON THE GREAT, THE MOTHER OF HARLOTS AND ABOMINATIONS OF THE EARTH.

—REVELATION 17:1–5

Sonnet XIII

I saw a woman sitting on a beast
Before mine eyes, of orange color hue:
Horror and dreadful name of blasphemy
Filled her with pride. And seven heads I saw,
Ten horns also the stately beast did bear.
She seemed with glory of the scarlet fair,
And with fine pearl and gold puffed up in heart.
The wine of whoredom in a cup she bare.
The name of Mystery writ in her face.
The blood of martyrs dear were her delight.
Most fierce and fell this woman seemed to me.
An angel then descending down from Heaven,
With thundering voice cried out aloud, and said,
Now for a truth great Babylon is fallen.

——EDMUND SPENSER

Let us be glad and rejoice, and give honour to him:
for the marriage of the Lamb is come, and his wife
hath made herself ready. And to her was granted
that she should be arrayed in fine linen, clean and
white: for the fine linen is the righteousness of
saints. And he saith unto me, Write, Blessed are
they which are called unto the marriage supper of
the Lamb. And he saith unto me, These are the
true sayings of God.

——REVELATION 19:7–9

Love (III)

Love bade me welcome: yet my soul drew back,
    Guiltie of dust and sinne.
But quick-ey'd Love, observing me grow slack
    From my first entrance in,
Drew nearer to me, sweetly questioning,
    If I lack'd any thing.

A guest, I answer'd, worthy to be here:
    Love said, You shall be he.
I the unkinde, ungratefull? Ah my deare,
    I cannot look on thee.
Love took my hand, and smiling did reply,
    Who made the eyes but I?

Truth Lord, but I have marr'd them: let my shame
    Go where it doth deserve.
And know you not, sayes Love, who bore the blame?
    My deare, then I will serve.
You must sit down, sayes Love, and taste my meat:
    So I did sit and eat.

——GEORGE HERBERT

St. Agnes' Eve

Deep on the convent-roof the snows
Are sparkling to the moon:
My breath to heaven like vapour goes:
May my soul follow soon!
The shadows of the convent-towers
    Slant down the snowy sward,

Still creeping with the creeping hours
    That lead me to my Lord:

Make Thou my spirit pure and clear
    As are the frosty skies,
Or this first snowdrop of the year
    That in my bosom lies

As these white robes are soil'd and dark,
    To yonder shining ground;
As this pale taper's earthly spark,
To yonder argent round;
So shows my soul before the Lamb,
    My spirit before Thee;
So in mine earthly house I am,
    To that I hope to be.
Break up the heavens, O Lord! and far,
    Thro' all yon starlight keen,
Draw me, thy bride, a glittering star,
    In raiment white and clean.

He lifts me to the golden doors;
    The flashes come and go;
All heaven bursts her starry floors,
    And strows her lights below,
And deepens on and up! the gates
Roll back, and far within
For me the Heavenly Bridegroom waits,
    To make me pure of sin.
The sabbaths of Eternity,
    One sabbath deep and wide—
A light upon the shining sea—
    The Bridegroom with his bride!

—ALFRED, LORD TENNYSON

Marvel of Marvels

Marvel of marvels, if I myself shall behold
With mine own eyes my King in his city of gold;
Where the least of lambs is spotless white in the fold,
Where the least and last of saints in spotless white is
stoled,
Where the dimmest head beyond a moon is aureoled.
O saints, my beloved, now mouldering to mould in
the mould,
Shall I see you lift your heads, see your cerements
unrolled,
See with these very eyes? who now in darkness and
cold
Tremble for the midnight cry, the rapture, the tale
untold,—
"The Bridegroom cometh, cometh, His Bride to
enfold."
Cold it is, my beloved, since your funeral bell was
tolled:
Cold it is, O my King, how cold alone on the wold.

—CHRISTINA GEORGINA ROSSETTI

And I saw heaven opened, and behold a white
horse; and he that sat upon him was called Faithful
and True, and in righteousness he doth judge and
make war. His eyes were as a flame of fire, and on
his head were many crowns; and he had a name
written, that no man knew, but he himself. And he
was clothed with a vesture dipped in blood: and his
name is called The Word of God. And the armies

which were in heaven followed him upon white
horses, clothed in fine linen, white and clean. And
out of his mouth goeth a sharp sword, that with it
he should smite the nations: and he shall rule them
with a rod of iron: and he treadeth the winepress
of the fierceness and wrath of Almighty God. And
he hath on his vesture and on his thigh a name written, KING OF KINGS, AND LORD OF LORDS.

—REVELATION 19:11–16

Battle Hymn of the Republic

Mine eyes have seen the glory of the coming of the
    Lord:
He is trampling out the vintage where the grapes of
    wrath are stored;
He hath loosed the fateful lightning of His terrible
    swift sword:
  His truth is marching on.

I have seen Him in the watch-fires of a hundred
    circling camps;
They have builded Him an altar in the evening dews
    and damps;
I can read His righteous sentence by the dim and
    flaring lamps:
  His day is marching on.

I have read a fiery gospel writ in burnished rows of
    steel:
"As ye deal with my contemners, so with you my
    grace shall deal;

Let the Hero, born of woman, crush the serpent with
  his heel,
    Since God is marching on."

He has sounded forth the trumpet that shall never call
  retreat;
He is sifting out the hearts of men before His
  judgment-seat;
Oh, be swift, my soul, to answer Him! be jubilant,
  my feet!
    Our God is marching on.

In the beauty of the lilies Christ was born across the
  sea,
With a glory in His bosom that transfigures you and
  me:
As He died to make men holy, let us die to make men
  free,
    While God is marching on.

—JULIA WARD HOWE

Sonnet XIV

Then might I see upon a white horse set
The faithful man with flaming countenance,
His head did shine with crowns set thereupon.
The word of God made him a noble name.
His precious robe I saw embrewed with blood.
Then saw I from the heaven on horses white,
A puissant army come the self-same way.
Then cried a shining angel as me thought,
That birds from air descending down on earth

Should war upon the kings, and eat their flesh.
Then did I see the beast and kings also
Joining their force to slay the faithful man.
But this fierce hateful beast and all her train,
Is pitiless thrown down in pit of fire.

—EDMUND SPENSER

And I saw a new heaven and a new earth: for the
first heaven and the first earth were passed away;
and there was no more sea. And I John saw the holy
city, new Jerusalem, coming down from God out
of heaven, prepared as a bride adorned for her husband. And I heard a great voice out of heaven saying, Behold, the tabernacle of God is with men,
and he will dwell with them, and they shall be his
people, and God himself shall be with them, and be
their God.

—REVELATION 21:1–3

The Voice of the Soul

O Lady! we receive but what we give,
And in our life alone does Nature live:
Ours is her wedding-garment, ours her shroud!
　And would we aught behold, of higher worth,
Than that inanimate cold world allowed
To the poor loveless ever-anxious crowd,
　Ah! from the soul itself must issue forth
A light, a glory, a fair luminous cloud

Enveloping the Earth—
And from the soul itself must there be sent
    A sweet and potent voice of its own birth,
Of all sweet sounds the life and element.
O pure of heart! thou need'st not ask of me
What this strong music in the soul may be!
What, and wherein it doth exist,
This light, this glory, this fair luminous mist,
This beautiful and beauty-making power.

    Joy, virtuous Lady! Joy that ne'er was given
Save to the pure, and in their purest hour,
Life and life's effluence, cloud at once and shower.
Joy, Lady! is the spirit and the power
Which wedding Nature to us gives in dower,
    A new Earth and a new Heaven,
Undreamt of by the sensual and the proud—
Joy is the sweet voice, Joy the luminous cloud—
    We in ourselves rejoice!
And thence flows all that charms or ear or sight,
    All melodies the echo of that voice,
All colours a suffusion from that light.

—SAMUEL TAYLOR COLERIDGE
(from *Dejection: an Ode*)

And there came unto me one of the seven angels
which had the seven vials full of the seven last
plagues, and talked with me, saying, Come hither,
I will shew thee the bride, the Lamb's wife. And he
carried me away in the spirit to a great and high
mountain, and shewed me that great city, the holy

Jerusalem, descending out of heaven from God, having the glory of God: and her light was like unto a stone most precious, even like a jasper stone, clear as crystal.

—REVELATION 21:9–11

And Did Those Feet

And did those feet in ancient time
Walk upon England's mountains green?
And was the holy Lamb of God
On England's pleasant pastures seen?

And did the Countenance Divine
Shine forth upon our clouded hills?
And was Jerusalem builded here
Among these dark Satanic Mills?

Bring me my bow of burning gold:
Bring me my Arrows of desire:
Bring me my Spear: O clouds unfold!
Bring me my Chariot of fire.

—WILLIAM BLAKE

And the twelve gates were twelve pearls; every several gate was of one pearl: and the street of the city was pure gold, as it were transparent glass.

—REVELATION 21:21

The Floor of Heaven

Here will we sit and let the sounds of music
Creep in our ears: soft stillness and the night
Become the touches of sweet harmony.
Sit, Jessica. Look how the floor of heaven
Is thick inlaid with patines of bright gold:
There's not the smallest orb which thou behold'st
But in his motion like an angel sings.

—WILLIAM SHAKESPEARE
(from *The Merchant of Venice*)

Sonnet XV

I saw new Earth, new Heaven, said Saint John.
And lo, the sea (quoth he) is now no more.
The holy City of the Lord, from high
Descendeth garnished as a loved spouse.
A voice then said, behold the bright abode
Of God and men. For he shall be their God.
And all their tears he shall wipe clean away.
Her brightness greater was than can be found.
Square was this city, and twelve gates it had.
Each gate was of an orient perfect pearl,
The houses gold, the pavement precious stone.
A lively stream, more clear than crystal is,
Ran through the mid, sprung from triumphant seat.
There grows life's fruit unto the Churches good.

—EDMUND SPENSER

And he shewed me a pure river of water of life, clear as crystal, proceeding out of the throne of God and of the Lamb.

——REVELATION 22:1

⚜

The River of God

It runs in the midst of the valleys to water the humble and the lowly. Wherefore they that thirst and would drink are bid to come down to the waters. They are common, but you must come to them— to where they are—or you will be nothing the better for them.

As this river is said to be pure, so it is said to be clear. Clear is to be taken for light, daylight, sunlight; for, indeed, it is never day nor sunshine with the soul until the streams of this river come gliding to our doors, into our houses, into our hearts. Clear is set in opposition to that which is not pleasing; for to be clear is to be pleasant. I read of rivers that looked red as blood, that stank like the blood of a dead man; but this is no such river. I read of rivers whose streams are like the streams of brimstone, fiery streams, streams of burning pitch; but this is none of them.

These are the waters that the doves love to sit by; because by the clearness of these streams they can see their pretty selves, as in a glass. These are the streams where the doves wash their eyes, and by which they solace themselves and take great content. As in fair waters a man may see the body

of the sun, and of the moon, and of the stars and
the very body of heaven; so he that stands upon the
bank of this river, and that washes his eyes with this
water, may see the Son of God, the glory of God
and the habitation that God has prepared for his
people. Are not these pleasant sights? Is not this
excellent water? Has not this river pleasant
streams?

There are many, now-a-days, that are for invent-
ing waters to drink for the health of the body; and
to allure those that are ill to buy, they will praise
their waters beyond their worth. Yea, and if they
are helpful to one person in a hundred, they make
as if they could cure every one. Well, here you have
the great Physician himself with his water, and he
calls it the water of life—water of life to the soul.
This water is *probatum est*. It has been proved times
without number; it never fails but when it is not
taken. No disease comes amiss to it; it cures blind-
ness, deadness, deafness, dumbness; it will drive
away devils and spirits; it will cure enchantments
and witchcrafts; it will dissolve doubts and mis-
trusts, though they are grown as hard as stone in
the heart. It will make you have a white soul, and
that is better than to have a white skin.

This river is the running out of God's heart. This
is his heart and soul. Wherefore forbear thy mis-
trusts, cast off thy slavish fears, hang thy misgivings
as to this upon the hedge; and believe thou hast an
invitation sufficient thereto. A river is before thy
face. And as to thy want of goodness and works, let
that by no means daunt thee. This is a river of water

of life—streams of grace and mercy. There is
enough therein to help thee, for grace brings all
that is wanting to the soul. Thou, therefore, hast
nothing to do but to drink and live for ever.

—JOHN BUNYAN
(from *The Water of Life*)

And the Spirit and the bride say, Come. And let
him that heareth say, Come. And let him that is
athirst come. And whosoever will, let him take the
water of life freely.

—REVELATION 22:17

The Dawning

Ah! what time wilt thou come? when shall that cry,
   "The Bridegroom's coming!" fill the sky?
   Shall it in the evening run
   When our words and works are done?
   Or will thy all-surprising light
     Break at midnight,
   When either sleep or some dark pleasure
   Possesseth mad man without measure?
   Or shall these early fragrant hours
     Unlock thy bowers,
   And with their blush of light descry
   Thy locks crowned with eternity?
   Indeed it is the only time
   That with thy glory doth best chime:

All now are stirring, every field
   Full hymns doth yield,
The whole creation shakes off night,
And for thy shadow looks the light;
Stars now vanish without number,
Sleepy planets set, and slumber,
The pursy clouds disband, and scatter;
All expect some sudden matter,
Not one beam triumphs, but from far
   That morning-star.

O at what time soever thou,
Unknown to us, the heavens wilt bow,
And with thy angels in the van
Descend to judge poor careless man,
Grant, I may not like puddle lie
In a corrupt security
Where, if a traveller water crave,
He finds it dead, and in a grave.
But as this restless vocal spring
All day and night doth run, and sing,
And though here born, yet is acquainted
Elsewhere, and flowing keeps untainted;
So let me all my busy age
In thy free services engage,
And though, while here, of force I must
Have commerce sometimes with poor dust,
And in my flesh, though vile, and low,
As this doth in her channel flow,
Yet let my course, my aim, my love
And chief acquaintance be above;
So when that day and hour shall come

In which thyself will be the sun,
Thou'lt find me dressed and on my way
Watching the break of thy great day.

——HENRY VAUGHAN

Paradise Re-entered

Through the strait gate of passion,
Between the bickering fire
Where flames of fierce love tremble
On the body of fierce desire:

To the intoxication,
The mind, fused down like a bead,
Flees in its agitation
The flames' stiff speed:

At last to calm incandescence,
Burned clean by remorseless hate,
Now, at the day's renascence
We approach the gate.

Now, from the darkened spaces
Of fear, and of frightened faces,
Death, in our awed embraces
Approached and passed by;

We near the flame-burnt porches
Where the brands of the angels, like torches,
Whirl,——in these perilous marches
Pausing to sigh;

We look back on the withering roses,
The stars, in their sun-dimmed closes,

Where 'twas given us to repose us
Sure on our sanctity;

Beautiful, candid lovers,
Burnt out of our earthly covers,
We might have nestled like plovers
In the fields of eternity.

There, sure in sinless being,
All-seen, and then all-seeing,
In us life unto death agreeing,
We might have lain.

But we storm the angel-guarded
Gates of the long discarded
Garden, which God has hoarded
Against our pain.

The Lord of Hosts and the Devil
Are left on Eternity's level
Field, and as victors we travel
To Eden home.

Back beyond good and evil
Return we. Eve dishevel
Your hair for the bliss-drenched revel
On our primal loam.

—D. H. LAWRENCE

For I testify unto every man that heareth the words
of the prophecy of this book, If any man shall add
unto these things, God shall add unto him the
plagues that are written in this book: And if any

man shall take away from the words of the book of this prophecy, God shall take away his part out of the book of life, and out of the holy city, and from the things which are written in this book. He which testifieth these things saith, Surely I come quickly. Amen.

—REVELATION 22:18–20

Johnny Appleseed's Hymn to the Sun

Christ the dew in the clod,
    Christ the sap of the trees,
Christ the light in the waterfall,
    Christ the soul of the sun,
Innermost blood of the sun,
    Grant I may touch the fringes
Of the outermost robe of the sun;
    Let me store your rays till my ribs
Carry the breath of lightning,
    Till my lips speak the fulness of thunder
To waken world-weary men:
    Till my whisper engenders lions
Out of the desert weeds.

Give me your eyes, O sun,
    To watch through the universe
Where other suns speed on,
    Brothers, children of God,
Mating the great deeps fair.

Take me unto yourself.
    My flesh is a sacrifice,

If only my soul may go
    As a flame to the edge of the sky
Where the sin-born stars come forth
    From the black strong chaos-sea,
From the infinite widths of night.

Grant that I may die in a star
    As the chosen of God all die
Rising again in the dreams
    Of sinning, star born men,
Destroying their sins forever.

Give me your hidden wings,
    That I may go to the heights
Of the gold-built cliffs of heaven,
    Where jungles in silence reign.
Where the streets, knee-deep in moss
    And the mansions heavy with trees
With Cedars of Lebanon
    With olive and orange and palm
Are silent but for the wind,
    Empty, mysterious.

Give me your strength, O sun!
    Give me your hidden wings,
Till I climb to the holiest place,
    That highest plain of all,
With its glassy shallow pools,
    That desert of level fear
Where three great thrones stand high
    Hewn from three ancient mountains,
Blind thrones of a fair lost land.
    You have left your thrones for the suns,

Great God, O Trinity,
    With all your marvelous hosts,
Cherubim, seraphim,
    You blaze in our eyes by day.
They gleam from the stars by night.

Give us your life, O sun!
    Body and blood of Christ,
Wafer of awful fire
    Give us the contrite heart,
Take out the death from us.

Either the dead are dead,
    Or today is eternity,
Your face is eternity,
    Your rays are our endless life.
You are girt with a golden girdle,
    You are with all your crucified
Angels and saints and men
    Who die under clouds in the stars:
You are bringing them back from the dead.
    They breathe on my face as I pray.

Give me your innermost life.
    Come quickly, Alpha, Omega,
Our God, the beginning and end!

—VACHEL LINDSAY

The Last Day

When the sun is withered up,
And the stars from Heaven roll;
When the mountains quake,

And ye let stray your she-camels, gone ten months in
    foal;
When wild beasts flock
With the people and the cattle
In terror, in amazement,
And the seas boil and rattle;
And the dead souls
For their bodies seek;
And the child vilely slain
Is bid to speak,
Being asked, "Who killed thee, little maid?
Tell us his name?"
While the books are unsealed,
And crimson flame
Flayeth the skin of the skies,
And Hell breaks ablaze;
And Paradise
Opens her beautiful gates to the gaze;—
Then shall each soul
Know the issues of the whole,
And the balance of its scroll.
Shall We swear by the stars
Which fade away?
By the Night drowned in darkness,
By the dead Day?
We swear not! a true thing is this;
It standeth sure,
He saw it and he heard, and Our word
Will endure!

When the sky cleaves asunder,
And the stars

Are scattered; and in thunder
All the bars
Of the seas burst, and all the graves are emptied
Like chests upturned,
Each soul shall see her doings, done and undone,
And what is earned.
The smiting, the smiting
Of that Day!
The horror, the splendor,
Who shall say?
The Day when none shall answer for his brother;
The Day which is with God, and with none other.

——SIR EDWIN ARNOLD

The Second Coming

Turning and turning in the widening gyre
The falcon cannot hear the falconer;
Things fall apart; the centre cannot hold;
Mere anarchy is loosed upon the world,
The blood-dimmed tide is loosed, and everywhere
The ceremony of innocence is drowned;
The best lack all conviction, while the worst
Are full of passionate intensity.

Surely some revelation is at hand;
Surely the Second Coming is at hand.
The Second Coming! Hardly are those words out
When a vast image out of *Spiritus Mundi*
Troubles my sight: somewhere in sands of the desert
A shape with lion body and the head of a man,
A gaze blank and pitiless as the sun,

Is moving its slow thighs, while all about it
Reel shadows of the indignant desert birds.
The darkness drops again; but now I know
That twenty centuries of stony sleep
Were vexed to nightmare by a rocking cradle,
And what rough beast, its hour come round at last,
Slouches towards Bethlehem to be born?

—WILLIAM BUTLER YEATS

The World's Last Night

The doctrine of the Second Coming teaches us that
we do not and cannot know when the world drama
will end. The curtain may be rung down at any
moment: say, before you have finished reading this
paragraph. This seems to some people intolerably
frustrating. So many things would be interrupted.
Perhaps you were going to get married next
month, perhaps you were going to get a raise next
week; you may be on the verge of a great scientif-
ic discovery; you may be maturing great social and
political reforms. Surely no good and wise God
would be so very unreasonable as to cut all this
short? Not now, of all moments!

But we think thus because we keep on assuming
that we know the play. We do not know the play. We
do not even know whether we are in Act I or Act V.
We do not know who are the major and who the
minor characters. The Author knows. The audience,
if there is an audience, (if angels and archangels and
all the company of heaven fill the pit and the stalls)

may have an inkling. But we, never seeing the play from outside, never meeting any characters except the tiny minority who are "on" in the same scenes as ourselves, wholly ignorant of the future and very imperfectly informed about the past, cannot tell at what moment the end ought to come. That it will come when it ought, we may be sure; but we waste our time in guessing when that will be. That it has a meaning we may be sure, but we cannot see it. When it is over, we may be told. We are led to expect that the Author will have something to say to each of us on the part that each of us has played. The playing it well is what matters infinitely.

The doctrine of the Second Coming, then, is not to be rejected because it conflicts with our favorite modern mythology. It is, for that very reason, to be the more valued and made more frequently the subject of meditation. It is the medicine our condition, especially, needs.

And with that, I turn to the practical. There is a real difficulty in giving this doctrine the place which it ought to have in our Christian life without, at the same time, running a certain risk. The fear of that risk probably deters many teachers who accept the doctrine from saying very much about it.

We must admit at once that this doctrine has, in the past, led Christians into very great follies. Apparently many people find it difficult to believe in this great event without trying to guess its date, or even without accepting as a certainty the date that any quack or hysteric offers them. To write a history of all these exploded predictions would need a book, and a sad, sordid, tragi-comical book it would be. One such prediction was circulating when St. Paul wrote his second letter to the Thessalonians. Someone had told them that "the Day" was "at hand." This was apparently having the result which such predictions usually have: people were idling and playing the busybody. One of the most famous predictions was that of poor William Miller in 1843. Miller (whom I take to have been an honest fanatic) dated the Second Coming to the year, the day, and the very minute. A timely comet fostered the delusion. Thousands waited for the Lord at midnight on March 21st, and went home to a late breakfast on the 22nd followed by the jeers of a drunkard.

Clearly, no one wishes to say anything that will reawaken such mass hysteria. We must never speak to simple, excitable people about "the Day" without emphasizing again and again the utter impossibility of prediction. We must try to show them that that impossibility is an essential part of the doctrine. If you do not believe our Lord's words, why do you believe in his return at all? And if you do believe them must you not put away from you, utterly and forever, any hope of dating that return? His teaching on the subject quite clearly consisted of three propositions: (1) That he will certainly return. (2) That we cannot possibly find out when. (3) And that therefore we must always be ready for him.

Note the therefore. Precisely because we cannot predict the moment, we must be ready at all

moments. Our Lord repeated this practical conclusion again and again; as if the promise of the
Return had been made for the sake of this conclusion alone. Watch, watch, is the burden of his
advice. I shall come like a thief. You will not, I most
solemnly assure you you will not, see me
approaching. If the householder had known at what
time the burglar would arrive, he would have been
ready for him. If the servant had known when his
absent employer would come home, he would not
have been found drunk in the kitchen. But they
didn't. Nor will you. Therefore you must be ready
at all times. The point is surely simple enough.

—C. S. LEWIS

BIOGRAPHICAL NOTES

Louisa May Alcott (1832–1888) was one of four daughters in a household very like the one she described in *Little Women*. Her father, a philosopher, was unable to support his family, so Louisa set herself to doing so—as a housemaid, seamstress, and teacher. But her creative energies were dedicated to writing. In nature she found a vital sense of God's presence, which she said was "never to change through forty years of life's vicissitudes, but to grow stronger for the sharp discipline of poverty and pain, sorrow and success."

Dante Alighieri (1265–1321) achieved literary immortality with his *Divine Comedy*. In a time when men of learning wrote Latin as a matter of course, Dante chose the dialect of his native Tuscany and turned it into a literary language, which became classic Italian. His allegorical masterpiece takes the reader on a dream journey through the entire universe of humanity and God—Hell, Purgatory, and Paradise. The end of the pilgrimage is a vision of God and the merging of the individual will in His supreme love. Longfellow, in a sonnet prefacing his own translation of the *Commedia,* compares Dante's epic poem to a cathedral.

Hans Christian Andersen (1805–1875) is beloved for tender and humorous fairy tales like *The Snow Queen* and *The Emperor's New Clothes*. But, like his own *Ugly Duckling,* the young Dane seemed destined for the unhappiest of endings. His shoemaker father died when Hans was just a boy. Penniless, with only a rudimentary education, the youth made his way to Copenhagen with dreams of becoming an actor, or a singer, or a dancer. He failed at all three. Subsequent literary attempts, bankrolled by benefactors, fared little better. When all prospects seemed exhausted, the Danish public succumbed to the charm of his fables. The fame of Hans Christian Andersen spread quickly, first across Europe and then worldwide.

Maya Angelou (1928–) is a poet and playwright, author of ten books, including a best-selling autobiography, *I Know Why the Caged Bird Sings.* But her first career, after growing up in segregated rural Arkansas, was as an actress and dancer. Marriage to a South African freedom-fighter took her to Africa and launched her as a journalist and teacher. Angelou returned to America during the civil rights struggles of the 1960s to work with Dr. Martin Luther King Jr. She served in various honorary posts under Presidents Ford and Carter and read a poem at the 1992 inauguration of President Clinton.

Sir Edwin Arnold (1832–1904) combined poetic gifts, Sanskrit scholarship, and a journalist's interest in Eastern religions. The result was a trio of epic and reverent poems. *The Light of Asia,* which first won Arnold acclaim in Victorian England, dealt with the life and teaching of Buddha, *Pearls of the Faith* with Mohammed, *The Light of the World* with Jesus Christ. *The Song Celestial,* Arnold's verse translation of the *Bhagavad Gita,* acquainted thousands of Western readers with one of the celebrated texts of Hinduism.

W. H. Auden (1907–1973) is considered one of the most significant poets of the twentieth century. As an Oxford student, he joined a group of young leftist writers, among them Stephen Spender and Christopher

Isherwood. Wanting to oppose the Fascists during the Spanish Civil War, Auden volunteered as an ambulance driver. The poet immigrated to the United States in 1939, becoming a citizen in 1946. The postwar period also marks Auden's return to the Anglican Church of his youth and a Pulitzer Prize for poetry that embodies his renewed religious affirmation.

Hilaire Belloc (1870–1953), who was born outside of Paris to a French father and English mother, became one of England's greatest literary figures—so much so that the BBC interrupted all its programs to announce his death. An early school influence was the legendary Catholic philosopher John Henry Newman. Belloc graduated with top honors from Oxford but was denied a teaching post due to anti-Catholic prejudice. He successfully turned instead to writing, where his works include history, biography, poetry, fiction, travel, and social commentary. At the age of thirty-six Belloc won election to Parliament after a famous campaign defense of his faith before a largely Protestant audience.

William Blake (1757–1827), an artist and poet, was a deeply religious, if unconventional, Christian who had angelic visions as a child. The lyrical and mystical elements of his imagination were intimately mingled, both reflected in his magical engravings and melodious poems. Many regard his greatest artwork to be his illustrations for the book of Job. Blake's wife, Catherine, once said of him: "He is always in Paradise."

James Boswell (1740–1795) was educated at the University of Edinburgh and tried his hand at various literary genres before finding his true calling as a biographer.

The subject was Samuel Johnson, thirty years Boswell's senior and widely celebrated for his *Dictionary*. For two decades Boswell and Johnson maintained a close companionship and steady correspondence. Boswell's journalistic account of those years—published, seven years after its subject's death, as the *Life of Samuel Johnson*—was generally acclaimed the greatest biography in English literature. Religion was one of many areas in which Boswell credited Johnson's influence. Johnson, Boswell wrote, helped him become "a rational Christian."

Emily Brontë (1818–1848) was a clergyman's daughter. She and her two sisters, Charlotte and Anne, all read voraciously. Though they lived a quiet country life, their soaring imaginations produced an amazing literary output of novels and poems. Emily, who wrote *Wuthering Heights,* lived in seclusion on her beloved moors and died of tuberculosis.

Rupert Brooke (1887–1915) came to represent an entire generation of idealistic English youth that was lost, either in death or total disillusionment, in the First World War. Educated at Rugby and Cambridge, Brooke was as noted for his physical beauty as his intellectual gifts—"a golden young Apollo" was one appraisal. The young poet traveled extensively in Europe, North America, and the South Seas before seeing war duty in Belgium and the Mediterranean. He died of fever on the Greek island of Skyros.

John Bunyan (1628–1688), the son of a tinker, was an unlearned genius who, after the death of his first wife, began serious study of the Bible while remaining ignorant of most secular literature. Yet *The Pilgrim's Progress,* written during the second of two prison terms for "unlicensed preaching," reached a larger audience than that attained by any contemporary man of letters. Indeed, *The Pilgrim's Progress* became almost a second Bible, translated into more than a hundred languages and dialects. A dream allegory like Dante's *Divine Comedy,* Bunyan's fable depicts the struggles and final triumph of the Christian life.

Edward Carpenter (1844–1929) has been called the English Walt Whitman, and with ample reason. Carpenter credited Whitman's *Leaves of Grass,* which he read almost continuously for ten years, for transfiguring his life. He had graduated from Cambridge and was ordained a curate in a local church. But Whitman's ecstatic verse prompted Carpenter not only to attempt his own free-form poetry, but to relinquish his college appointments and holy orders, indeed to resign his social rank in order to live humbly. *Towards Democracy,* almost eerily Whitmanesque in style, gained a considerable following for many years. In 1884, on a pilgrimage to America, Carpenter paid personal homage to his mentor.

Geoffrey Chaucer (1340–1400), the son of a prosperous London vintner, had a storybook-heroic youth—war prisoner in France and diplomat in the king's service in Italy. These foreign adventures exposed him to French and Italian literature, both of which profoundly affected his poetic style. His masterwork, *Canterbury Tales,* encompasses sketches of travelers on a religious pilgrimage. A committed Christian, Chaucer saw the world as a ladder ascending toward God.

G. K. Chesterton (1874–1936) won a London school-boy's "Milton" prize for splendid verse. The grown-up

Gilbert Keith Chesterton, however, earned his keep as a freelance journalist, reviewing books and working in a publisher's office, while churning out fiction, poetry, and criticism. An interesting literary outgrowth of Chesterton's middle-aged conversion to Catholicism was the fictional Father Brown, who, in a celebrated series of crime novels, combines his sleuthing with sermonizing.

Samuel Taylor Coleridge (1772–1834) was raised at his father's vicarage in Devonshire, England. At three he could read the Bible, and the *Arabian Nights* before he was five. An early plan to become a Unitarian minister was abandoned when he fell under the spell of opium (poems such as "Kubla Khan" mirror his drugged imagination). Coleridge recovered his Christian faith later in life and was esteemed a great religious thinker. He died in communion with the Church of England.

Richard Crashaw (1613–1649) was influenced by George Herbert to express his genius in religious verse. But the young man had inherited a passion for both theology and poetry from his clergyman father. During the civil strife in England, Crashaw fled to France, where eventually, though raised a fierce "antipapist," he embraced Catholicism. His religious and secular poems were collected by a friend and published anonymously during his exile. The poet died in Italy at the age of thirty-six in the service of a cardinal.

E E Cummings (1894–1962) delighted in being the bad boy of American poetry. He was born in Cambridge, Massachusetts, where his father was a Harvard professor and an ordained minister. After his own Harvard studies, young Edward Estlin rushed off to Europe—World War I was breaking out—to serve in the ambulance corps. His first volume of poems, appearing when he was thirty, gained notoriety for its unusual rhythms and lack of uppercase letters. And yet, despite this linguistic and typographical playfulness, Cummings's poetry betrays his Unitarian and transcendental heritage—and ultimately celebrates a vision of a redeemed world.

Walter de la Mare (1873–1956) began publishing pseudonymous poetry while working for Standard Oil in London. While his business career lasted for twenty years, his literary endeavors continued half a century, during which he composed or edited more than forty volumes—poetry, novels, short stories, anthologies. De la Mare's writing reflects what he termed "visionary moments," a heightened experience just beyond day-to-day reality.

René Descartes (1596–1650) was a French philosopher whose championing of intellectual inquiry marked the transition from the Middle Ages to the modern world. His influence on philosophy and mathematics—indeed, on all of modern science—was immense. Cartesian philosophy is often reduced to his famous axiom: "I think, therefore I am." Using similar logic, Descartes asserted that God must exist, otherwise an imperfect being (humankind) could not conceive of a perfect Being. Though condemned by some as an atheist, the truth is that Descartes never wavered from the faith instilled by the Jesuit teachers of his youth.

Charles Dickens (1812–1870) once recalled as a child looking downstairs at people celebrating New Year's Day and seeing "a very long row of ladies and gentlemen sitting against a wall, all drinking at once out of little glass cups with handles, like custard cups . . . [It was] very like my first idea of the good people in Heaven." Even without his many beloved novels, Dickens's literary fame would have been assured by his poignant fable of repentance, *A Christmas Carol*. Less well known is a little volume he penned for his children, *The Life of Our Lord*.

Emily Dickinson (1830–1886) died in the house where she was born in Amherst, Massachusetts, a profoundly Christian New England town. After brief schooling, she settled into seclusion, probably because of an unhappy love affair, which she ended because she could not "wreck another woman's life." Almost completely withdrawn from life, Emily would not allow family or friends to publish her poetry during her lifetime. After Emily's death, her sister found more than a thousand poems hidden in boxes and drawers, some in hand-stitched booklets, others penned on the backs of old envelopes and shopping lists. These ingenious works reflect a mystical love of God. Her life was celebrated in the 1976 play *The Belle of Amherst*.

John Donne (1572–1631) was born into a family of staunch Catholics, with two Jesuit uncles. But when he came of age, he rejected Catholicism to embrace the Anglican Church. In straitened circumstances, with a sickly wife and seven children, he was pressured by King James to take religious orders. His first sermon before the king reportedly carried his audience "to heaven, in holy raptures." His poems reflect the struggle between spirit and flesh, individual faith and general disillusionment.

Fyodor Dostoevsky (1821–1881), by vast reading, overcame a meager education. He was a promising young novelist when involvement with Russian political reformers led to his arrest. He was sentenced to be shot and was actually facing the firing squad when the czar's courier arrived, commuting the punishment to four years hard labor. This terrifying experience, and his imprisonment in Siberia, kindled Dostoevsky's compassion for all who suffer and made real to him the need for Christ's saving grace. His last novel, *The Brothers Karamazov*, dramatizes the search for God.

John Dryden (1631–1700) was made Poet Laureate of England in 1668 but afterward wrote almost exclusively for the stage. Raised in a Puritan family, he attacked Roman Catholics in the play *The Spanish Friar*. But in a spiritual turnabout, his search for what he termed an "infallible creed" ultimately led him to convert to Catholicism.

George Eliot (1819–1880) was the pen name of English novelist Mary Ann Evans. Early and severe religious training did not dampen her spiritual idealism. She excelled at music and had an insatiable appetite for reading. At boarding school, Evans led prayer meetings among the girls and organized charitable enterprises. In her early twenties she studied Greek and Hebrew and translated a German theologian's *Life of Jesus*. Her novels—*Silas Marner, Adam Bede, Mill on the Floss*—are full of tributes to Christian virtue.

T. S. Eliot (1888–1965), born in St. Louis, Missouri, to a distinguished Boston family that founded Washington University, stayed on in England after his Oxford years.

His ingenious poetry, especially after publication of *The Waste Land,* created a literary sensation on both sides of the Atlantic; and ultimately won him the Nobel prize. After 1927, when Eliot became a British subject and joined the Anglican Church, both his poems and plays reflected his search for spiritual meaning, with frequent allusions to religious literature. As Ezra Pound once chided, Eliot began to prefer "Moses to the Muses."

Ralph Waldo Emerson (1803–1882) counted among his ancestors seven ministers, and his father led the First Unitarian Church in Boston. Emerson became a minister but, after his wife's death, struggled with depression and chafed under rigid doctrine. His subsequent transcendentalism, embodied in eloquent essays and poems, preaches the virtues of self-reliance, optimism, serenity, and faith in the God who dwells within. "For the soul, let redemption be sought," Emerson wrote. "Cast conformity behind you and acquaint men at first hand with Deity."

Edward FitzGerald (1809–1883) is the translator of the *Rubáiyát of Omar Khayyám,* to most English readers the best known of all Oriental poems. It has been said that these haunting quatrains, full of luxurious fatalism, owe much more to FitzGerald than Khayyám, an obscure eleventh-century Persian mystic, but the translator deliberately left his name off the first printing. And, after Rossetti and Swinburne helped the *Rubáiyát* become a literary sensation in Victorian England, the modest FitzGerald yearned for a return to anonymity, preferring a secluded life among his Cambridge University friends, among whom he numbered Tennyson and Thackeray.

C. S. Forester (1899–1966) was born in Cairo, the son of a British army officer, and educated in London, where he studied medicine. After service as an infantryman in World War I, Forester abandoned medicine in favor of literature. His efforts at poetry were unavailing, but his first novel, *Payment Deferred,* enjoyed great acclaim and was later dramatized and filmed with Charles Laughton. Other successful fiction followed, notably *The African Queen.* In 1937, Forester published *Beat to Quarters* about an intrepid British naval captain during the Napoleonic wars. Forester went on to write ten more titles in the saga of Horatio Hornblower, establishing a swashbuckling historical genre, which other writers, most notably Patrick O'Brian, have perpetuated.

Robert Frost (1874–1963) was born in San Francisco, though his ancestry was strictly New England. After his father's death when Frost was only ten, his mother returned east to settle in Lawrence, Massachusetts. A poet herself with deep religious convictions, she nurtured her son's poetic gifts and fostered the rich vein of mysticism and symbolism that permeates his "talky" blank verse. Frost once wrote that when he was a boy he often held his hands over his ears and buried his face "to drown out the mystical voices calling to him." Before "overnight success" and four Pulitzer Prizes arrived in his later years, Frost had tried his hand at teaching school, making shoes, editing a weekly paper, and farming.

Johann Wolfgang von Goethe (1749–1832) had a passion for poetry as early as age eight. At nine he built an altar and developed his own mystical religion, in hopes of approaching God directly. At thirteen he studied Hebrew and read much of the Bible, while his secular studies encompassed literature, science, law, medicine—indeed, the whole of human learning. At the University of Leipzig young Goethe wrote verses in German, French, English, and Italian. He went on to achieve such international eminence with his voluminous works that Thomas Carlyle proclaimed him "the teacher and exemplar of his age."

Oliver Goldsmith (1728–1774) at the age of twenty-one applied for ordination as a Protestant minister. Due perhaps to his penchant for gaudy clothes and frivolous occupations like singing and playing cards, he was rejected. After failing at several other professions, Goldsmith turned to writing as a "booksellers' hack," doing translations, reviews, and children's books. But his literary genius quickly attracted popular attention. *The Vicar of Wakefield* was more widely read than any other eighteenth-century fiction, with the possible exception of *Robinson Crusoe,* and Goldsmith's most popular play, *She Stoops to Conquer,* has remained on the stage for more than two centuries.

Bret Harte (1836–1902) was born in New York but found his life's work in California, where he arrived as a young man a few years after the Gold Rush began. A series of odd jobs led Harte into newspaper work, first as a printer, then as a writer of poems, parodies, and humorous short stories. He struck it rich by mining the pioneer life for the entertainment of readers back east. Most popular among his works are *The Luck of Roaring Camp* and *The Outcast of Poker Flats.*

George Herbert (1593–1633) was profoundly influenced by his mother, a friend of John Donne. Herbert taught briefly at Cambridge, where he had been educated. When an attempt to succeed at court failed, however, he determined "to lose himself in an humble way" and take priestly orders. He loved the Church of England and held services twice a day at his parish in Salisbury. Like his mentor, Donne, Herbert found spiritual inspiration in everyday objects. He is noted for his pious and playful poetry.

Robert Herrick (1591–1674) was the son of a London goldsmith. He took a small vicarage near Devonshire and celebrated the rural customs in his village. Though his sermons were termed "florid and witty," Herrick, who never married, is far better known for his pastoral love poems.

Oliver Wendell Holmes (1809–1894), a physician and professor at Harvard Medical School, abandoned medicine for poetry and prose. His father was a minister of the Congregational Church, but Holmes later turned to Unitarianism. He earned the title of "The Autocrat of the Breakfast Table" through clever essays under that title. Holmes had briefly studied law at Harvard, but his real contribution to jurisprudence was his son, Oliver Jr., who became the greatest Supreme Court justice of his era.

Homer is the name forever linked with the *Iliad* and the *Odyssey,* arguably the greatest narrative poems ever written. But of the actual author almost nothing is known. Legend has him a "blind bard" who moved among the Greek cities of Asia Minor eight or nine centuries before Christ, collecting and reciting sagas of ancient gods and heroes. But the Homeric epics are more than grand adventure. Containing a profound moral dimension, they have been called the first tragedies. Athenian schoolboys studied them in the sixth century B.C., and they remain today a part of the classical curriculum.

Gerard Manley Hopkins (1844–1889) was born into a High Anglican family, but converted to Roman Catholicism at age twenty-two. Two years later he became a Jesuit and burned many of his spiritual-sensual poems, believing the religious life incompatible with creating poetry. Fortunately, much of his innovative work survived, allowing us to experience the depth and passion of his religious convictions.

Julia Ward Howe (1819–1910), born in New York City to a banker father and poetess mother, began writing verse in her childhood. She married a man who shared her strong social idealism. Together they published *The Commonwealth,* an antislavery paper, and made their Boston home a haven for abolitionists. A Civil War visit to a Union Army camp inspired Howe to write the stirring "Battle Hymn of the Republic," which first appeared in the *Atlantic Monthly* in 1862.

Victor Hugo (1802–1885) was for fifty years the greatest literary force in France. Before age six he had taught himself to read "by merely looking at the printed letters." And, at twenty-two, his literary reputation was already so great that he was made a Chevalier of the Legion of Honor. His poems and novels—the most celebrated is *Les Miserables*—exemplify the goodness of God, the triumph of life, and the power of redemption.

James Joyce (1882–1941) was educated in Jesuit boarding schools, graduating from University College,

Dublin. But Joyce rebelled violently against his Irish Catholic roots and schooling and had Stephen Dedalus, the hero of his autobiographical *A Portrait of the Artist as a Young Man,* do likewise, switching vocation from priest to writer. And yet all of Joyce's innovative fiction—including such complex and controversial masterworks as *Ulysses* and *Finnegan's Wake*—is informed with the religious fervor he publicly disdained.

John Keats (1795–1821) was apprenticed to a surgeon and obtained his license to practice medicine. But, as he turned twenty, a passion for poetry prompted him to set aside his medical training. His odes—among them "Ode to a Nightingale" and "Ode on a Grecian Urn"—are, in Keats's felicitous phrase, statements on the "holiness of the heart's affections and the truth of imagination." At twenty-six, Keats succumbed to tuberculosis, the disease that had taken both his mother and brother.

Rudyard Kipling (1865–1936) was born in Bombay and educated in English boarding schools. He returned to India at seventeen to take up journalism. Early verse made him popular, but his witty and worldly short stories, collected in *Plain Tales from the Hills,* created a literary sensation in 1890s' London. "Kipling is too clever to live," was Robert Louis Stevenson's admiring verdict. Though often criticized for celebrating British imperialism, Kipling has never been neglected. His classics—like the *Jungle Books* and *Captains Courageous*—delight generation after generation. He was awarded the 1907 Nobel prize.

D. H. Lawrence (1885–1930) was born to a working-class family in Nottinghamshire, England, the fourth child of a coal miner. His youthful struggles to escape the

mines through education are depicted in his autobiographical novel, *Sons and Lovers.* Despite ill health (he died
of tuberculosis at forty-four) and endless wanderings
with his wife, Frieda, Lawrence produced several novels,
including the scandalous *Lady Chatterley's Lover,* as well as
volumes on psychological and religious speculation. A
complex and tortured man, David Herbert Lawrence
used his poetry to examine sensual and spiritual perplex-
ities.

C. S. Lewis (1898–1963), an atheist into his thirties, had
a conversion experience—"surprised by joy," as he told
it—in a motorcycle sidecar en route to a zoo. Lewis
arrived at his destination convinced that Jesus Christ was
the Son of God. For the rest of his life, while pursuing a
distinguished academic career at Oxford and Cambridge,
Lewis proclaimed and defended what he deemed the
essentials of Christianity—in essays, sermons, and radio
broadcasts. His literary output embraces novels of science-
fiction and fantasy, poetry and literary criticism—more
than thirty books, all in print. His marriage to Joy
Davidman Gresham was dramatized in a 1993 movie,
Shadowlands. In 1998, the one-hundredth anniversary of
Lewis's birth was celebrated with a host of activities in
both England and the United States.

Vachel Lindsay (1879–1931), like Yeats, studied drawing and painting before turning to poetry. But Lindsay
was not content with simply writing and publishing
verse. He embarked on walking tours, reciting his lines
like an ancient minstrel in exchange for food and lodging.
The "vagabond poet" later reinvented himself as a vaude-
villian, chanting his rhythmic, religious verse to ragtime

musical accompaniment. In his heyday, Lindsay acquired a certain celebrity, and his rhapsodic poems, especially "The Congo," became well known. But the novelty soon wore off. At fifty-two, no longer in demand, the poet-performer took his own life.

Henry Wadsworth Longfellow (1807–1882) was born in Portland, Maine, to a generations-old New England family. As a boy he wrote prose and verse for newspapers and magazines, but, when his father frowned on his literary aspirations, he pursued an academic career in modern languages. Paramount among his many translations from European poets is his rendering of Dante's *Divine Comedy*. Ultimately, in spite of his father's skepticism, Longfellow attained renown for his own literary works, especially such narrative poems as *Hiawatha, The Courtship of Miles Standish,* and *Paul Revere's Ride,* and was the first American poet to receive a memorial in London's Westminster Abbey.

Christopher Marlowe (1564–1593) had a cometary career—brief, incandescent, full of mystery. He rose from humble beginnings; his father was a shoemaker, his grandfather a tanner. After winning a scholarship to Cambridge, Marlowe swiftly made a name for himself, not only as an ingenious poet, but for his reckless opinions. Controversy continued to swirl around him; in London he was arrested on mysterious charges. Then, at twenty-nine, Marlowe was dead, stabbed in a tavern brawl, leaving behind several masterpieces of lyric poetry and drama, works that stand comparison with those of Shakespeare. Though a self-proclaimed atheist at Cambridge, Marlowe achieved religious eloquence through his characters, especially in his greatest play, *The Tragical History of Doctor Faustus.*

Andrew Marvell (1621–1678) was born in his father's rectory (and grammar school) in Yorkshire, England, and educated there and at Trinity College. Known in his time more as a political satirist and pamphleteer, Marvell wrote "metaphysical" and "garden" poems that were circulated mostly in manuscript. When Milton was appointed Latin secretary under Oliver Cromwell, the great poet made Marvell his assistant. Marvell subsequently wrote an ode hailing Cromwell as Caesar, then adroitly changed his politics during the Restoration. Marvell's poetic standing was improved more than a century after his death, thanks to the praise of William Wordsworth and Charles Lamb.

Herman Melville (1819–1891) settled down to a comfortable life as a customs inspector on the New York docks in 1866—after a wildly adventurous youth. At age eighteen he had run away to sea. In the course of a whaling cruise in the Pacific, he was captured by cannibals in the Marquesas, then rescued by an Australian ship, which he left at Tahiti. Fortunately for posterity, Melville devoted the final twenty-five years of his life to literature. His masterpiece, *Moby Dick,* which was dedicated to his dear friend Nathaniel Hawthorne, portrays seafaring life with an unmatched vigor and originality.

John Milton (1608–1674) entered Cambridge with the idea of becoming a clergyman but abandoned it because, he wrote, "tyranny had invaded" the Church of England. He afterward devoted himself to scholarship and literature. Though profoundly religious and a genuine Christian who valued (and studied) the Bible over all other books, Milton no longer attended church. His masterwork, *Paradise Lost,* published when he was nearly sixty, describes Satan and his fallen angels warring with God and His angelic host.

Edgar Allan Poe (1809–1849), the son of actors, was orphaned at the age of three. Disappointments in love and an unconquerable attraction to liquor haunted his life and were reflected in his brooding stories. But Poe had as well a gentle, affectionate side, which appears in his idealistic, visionary poems. He died in an alcoholic stupor, whispering, "Lord, help my poor soul."

Alexander Pope (1688–1744) was the son of devotedly Catholic parents. He was his own tutor—not only in English, but in French, Italian, Latin, and Greek. He spent a dozen years on his famous translations of Homer's *Iliad* and *Odyssey*. At twenty-four he published a sacred poem, "Messiah." By twenty-five he was a fashionable poet and recognized wit, earning a prosperous living with his pen. His *Essay on Man* was a defense of religion on natural grounds. According to the priest who gave him the last rites, "Pope's mind was resigned and wrapt up in the love of God and man."

Sir Walter Raleigh (1552–1618) was the quintessential English Renaissance man—handsome courtier, soldier, sailor, statesman, explorer, and accomplished poet. He was also a man who made enemies. While imprisoned in the Tower of London under sentence of death, Raleigh wrote a *History of the World* for the instruction of the Prince of Wales. Released, he led an expedition to South America and returned voluntarily to be rearrested and finally executed. For Raleigh was also a man of abiding faith who went calmly to his death, having written and tucked into his Bible his own epitaph. It concluded: ". . . from this earth, this grave, this dust, My God shall raise me up, I trust."

Arthur Rimbaud (1854–1891) began at the age of ten to write dazzling poetry. But, before he was sixteen, the French lad had run away from home, a pattern that would repeat throughout his chaotic life. *A Season in Hell,* finished at nineteen, was Rimbaud's final work. He spent the balance of his life as a global vagabond, winding up in East Africa under another name. In Paris, meanwhile, Rimbaud had become a famous "dead poet."

Christina Georgina Rossetti (1830–1894) was so devoted to her High Anglican faith that she turned down a suitor who was "either not a Christian at all, or else he was a Christian of undefined or heterodox views." Committed to the heavenly Bridegroom, her solitary life produced a wealth of deeply spiritual creative works, marked by magical imagery, an angelic voice, and a love for nature.

Dante Gabriel Rossetti (1828–1882) was born into an impoverished but highly cultured household. His father, an eccentric professor of Italian, had highly original views on the poet Dante. The sensitive boy became a painter as well as a poet. His poetess sister Christina was the model for Rossetti's graceful painting of the Virgin Mary.

Jean-Paul Sartre (1905–1980) was born in Paris, where he lived and wrote all his life. Upon his death, eighty thousand people lined the streets of Paris to pay their last respects. Because of his philosophical treatises, essays, novels, and dramas, Sartre became synonymous with French Existentialism. Its central idea he expressed as the inescapable necessity for choice: "Man is condemned to be free." During World War II, the writer joined the Resistance; and during the Cold War he found his political sympathies with Marxism but later made a well-publicized break with the Communists. Awarded the 1964 Nobel prize for literature, Sartre declined to accept.

George Bernard Shaw (1856–1950) was a kaleidoscopic literary genius, earning acclaim as playwright, essayist, economist, political activist, lecturer, journalist, music critic, novelist, and prolific letter writer. Though his entertaining comedies and dramas have proved Shaw's enduring legacy, the breadth of his thought can also be traced in the provocative prefaces to those plays. "Shavian" philosophy, however, defies easy categorization. Though a founder of Fabian Socialism, George Bernard Shaw subsequently became a passionate foe of Darwinism and materialism. In the preface to *Back to Methuselah,* Shaw wrote that Western civilization could be saved only by a return to religion.

Edmund Spenser (1552–1599), the son of a London clothmaker, wrote and translated verse as a boy. He possessed the supreme poetic gifts of melody, rhythm, and image and is credited with crystallizing the forms and patterns of English verse. His masterwork, *The Faerie Queen,* is an elaborate allegory of twelve books (only six were completed), each narrating the exploits of a knight who symbolized one of the "morall vertues." Spenser was a sincere and militant Christian.

James Stephens (1882–1950) was doing clerical work in Dublin when his deceptively simple verses came to the attention of the poet George Russell ("AE"), who arranged publication. The book, steeped in Irish fantasy, was immediately popular, and its delightful prose sequel, a fairy-tale assortment entitled *The Crock of Gold,* earned Stephens even wider acclaim. His later poems wandered further afield from Irish folklore, into world religions and mystical experience.

Harriet Beecher Stowe (1811–1896) was, said Abraham Lincoln, "the little lady who caused this great war." Stowe's passionate belief in the abolition of slavery was expressed in *Uncle Tom's Cabin,* reflecting her deeply religious views. Her father, a strict Calvinist, headed a theological seminary in Cincinnati, Ohio, where Harriet attended school and married a professor. Five of her six brothers became ministers.

Jonathan Swift (1667–1745) could read any chapter in the Bible by the age of five. Born in Dublin to an English family, Swift was educated at Trinity College. In England at the age of twenty-seven, he became a clergyman. But prospects for clerical advancement were crippled by a satirical essay, *Tale of the Tub,* which took deadly aim on insincerity in literature and religion. Undaunted, Swift continued to dip his pen in his vitriol. Even his children's classic, *Gulliver's Travels,* with its Lilliputians and Yahoos, is a thinly veiled satire on human shams and shortcomings.

Alfred, Lord Tennyson (1809–1892) was the fourth of twelve children. Their father, an English clergyman, was also a skillful poet who supervised his children's schooling. Tennyson wrote verse at a precociously early age but passed much of his young manhood in poverty and melancholy. Only at the age of forty-one, when he was appointed Poet Laureate by Queen Victoria, did his reputation and the sales of his works soar. A devout and sensitive man, Tennyson said of his wife, "The peace of God came into my life before the altar when I wedded her."

Francis Thompson (1859–1907) was educated in the Catholic faith, studied medicine in college, failed his exams three times, and fled to London to seek his fortune. There, beset by ill health, miserably poor and lonely, he turned to opium. He was rescued by an insightful editor and found abundant consolation in religious ecstasy. Thompson wrote, "I would be the poet of the return to God." He spent his last years in Franciscan and Capuchin monasteries.

Leo Tolstoy (1828–1910), at the time of his death, was the pre-eminent man of letters in all the world. Yet, at the peak of his powers three decades before, he had renounced literature. The creator of *War and Peace* and *Anna Karenina* had spent the balance of his life in a search for moral and religious justification, not only studying the Gospels intensely, but teaching them to the village children on his country estate.

Thomas Traherne (1633–1674), the son of a shoemaker, was educated at Oxford, ordained in the Church of England, and appointed rector near his birthplace in Hereford, where he lived simply and austerely. Amazingly, none of his poems were published during his lifetime. In fact, more than two hundred years after his death, a manuscript of his was purchased for a few shillings by a scholar who assumed the poems were by Henry Vaughan. Further research revealed the author, who portrayed a childlike innocence and spiritual enchantment with everyday things, to be the minister Traherne.

Mark Twain (1835–1910) is still considered the most original of all American writers—"the Lincoln of our literature," according to his contemporary, the novelist William Dean Howells. Young Sam Clemens (Twain was a pen name) didn't let a lack of formal education stop him from acquiring an astonishing knowledge of the world. His boyhood home, Hannibal, Missouri, linked him with both the Middle West and the South. This, plus later tenures in California, New York, and Connecticut, along with frequent travels abroad, gave Twain an unmatched breadth of experience. His writing career began with newspaper work in Nevada and California, in which he demonstrated mastery of both humorous essays and foreign correspondence. But Twain's well-deserved literary eminence rests upon his beloved, humorous novels, *Huckleberry Finn* and *Tom Sawyer*.

Henry Vaughan (1622–1695), British poet and mystic, was born into an ancient Welsh family. Sent to London to study law, the young man instead became a physician. He published his first secular poetry at the age of twenty-four but later turned his attention to sacred subjects. In the preface to a book of spiritual poems, Vaughan thanked "the blessed man, Mr. George Herbert, whose holy life and verse gained many pious converts, of whom I am the least." His mystical view of nature affected William Wordsworth, who owned a copy of Vaughan's poems.

Virgil (70–19 B.C.), a friend of Augustus Caesar, wishing to compose a national epic, took as his subject the mythical founder of Rome, Aeneas, who was also one of the Trojan heroes of Homer's *Iliad*. The resulting epic poem, *The Aeneid,* has long been considered the greatest secular book of the Western world. It recounts not only Aeneas's wanderings after escaping the sack of Troy but his moral and spiritual journey as well. For Virgil, deriving his idea of good and evil from Platonic philosophy, deemed true heroism to be founded upon virtuous conduct. Like the Homeric epics, *The Aeneid* has been a mainstay of English and American literary education.

Walt Whitman (1819–1892) was the son of a Quaker father and deeply spiritual mother. His audacious prose and poetry championed the ideals of the transcendental period of American thought. Democracy's celebrator, Whitman believed his country's destiny was to be found in a rediscovery of the religious spirit.

John Greenleaf Whittier (1807–1892) was so closely connected to his faith that he was called the "Quaker Poet." Because of his staunch religious beliefs, he was a bitter enemy of slavery and used his creative energy to fuel abolition. Along with antislavery and pastoral New England poetry, Whittier wrote many hymns that are sung to this day.

Thornton Wilder (1897–1975) was essentially a moralist in his plays, something traceable in part to his morally upright father and Presbyterian minister grandfather. His inspirational novel, *The Bridge of San Luis Rey,* earned him a Pulitzer at the age of thirty-one. *Our Town,* which opened in 1938, remains America's most produced play, a touching and tender look at small-town life in a fictional New Hampshire town. "I am not interested in the ephemeral," Wilder once said, but "in those things that repeat and repeat and repeat in the lives of the millions."

William Wordsworth (1770–1850) found his three years at Cambridge of little intellectual profit. While his family hoped he would become a minister, the thought of "vegetating on a paltry curacy" had little appeal for the young man. Yet much of his delicate and intimate poetry is absorbed with divinity—and a "communion with nature," which he discovered as a child. Bereft after the death of his brother John, Wordsworth returned to the Anglican Church.

William Butler Yeats (1865–1939), the son of a well-known Dublin painter, studied the brush and oils but turned instead to pen and ink for capturing his artistic visions. After an early foray into London poetry circles, Yeats returned to his native Ireland, for which he would feel a lifelong devotion. Indeed, Yeats was credited with the renaissance of Irish culture, helping to establish the Gaelic League and Irish Literary Theater. He wrote dramas and lyrics about local legends, re-created Gaelic folklore, and even served as a senator. Yeats continued to write emotionally indelible verse until his death at seventy-three.